# THE PRACTITIONER INQUIRY SERIES

Marilyn Cochran-Smith and Susan L. Lytle, SERIES EDITORS

ADVISORY BOARD: JoBeth Allen, Judy Buchanan, Curt Dudley-Marling, Robert Fecho,
Sarah Freedman, Dixie Goswami, Joyce E. King, Sarah Michaels, Luis Moll,
Susan Noffke, Sharon Ravitch, Marty Rutherford, Lynne Strieb, Diane Waff, Ken Zeichner

---

Democratic Habits in the Art Classroom:
Supporting Student Voice, Choice, and Community
ELIZABETH SUTTON, ED.

Promising Pedagogies for Teacher Inquiry and Practice : Teaching Out Loud
KATHERINE CRAWFORD-GARRETT & DAMON R. CARBAJAL, EDS.

Autobiography on the Spectrum:
Disrupting the Autism Narrative
BETH A. MYERS

Repositioning Educational Leadership:
Practitioners Leading from an Inquiry Stance
JAMES H. LYTLE, SUSAN L. LYTLE, MICHAEL C. JOHANEK, & KATHY J. RHO, EDS.

Professional Development in Relational Learning Communities: Teachers in Connection
MIRIAM B. RAIDER-ROTH

Impactful Practitioner Inquiry: The Ripple Effect on Classrooms, Schools, and Teacher Professionalism
SUE NICHOLS & PHIL CORMACK

Teaching in Themes:
An Approach to Schoolwide Learning, Creating Community, and Differentiating Instruction
DEBORAH MEIER, MATTHEW KNOESTER, & KATHERINE CLUNIS D'ANDREA, EDS.

Family Dialogue Journals: School–Home Partnerships That Support Student Learning
JOBETH ALLEN, JENNIFER BEATY, ANGELA DEAN, JOSEPH JONES, STEPHANIE SMITH MATHEWS, JEN MCCREIGHT, ELYSE SCHWEDLER, & AMBER M. SIMMONS

Raising Race Questions:
Whiteness and Inquiry in Education
ALI MICHAEL

Making Space for Active Learning:
The Art and Practice of Teaching
ANNE C. MARTIN & ELLEN SCHWARTZ, EDS.

The First Year of Teaching: Classroom Research to Increase Student Learning
JABARI MAHIRI & SARAH WARSHAUER FREEDMAN, EDS.

A Critical Inquiry Framework for K–12 Teachers: Lessons and Resources from the U.N. Rights of the Child
JOBETH ALLEN & LOIS ALEXANDER, EDS.

Democratic Education in Practice:
Inside the Mission Hill School
MATTHEW KNOESTER

Action Research in Special Education:
An Inquiry Approach for Effective Teaching and Learning
SUSAN M. BRUCE & GERALD J. PINE

Inviting Families into the Classroom:
Learning from a Life in Teaching
LYNNE YERMANOCK STRIEB

Jenny's Story: Taking the Long View of the Child—Prospect's Philosophy in Action
PATRICIA F. CARINI & MARGARET HIMLEY, WITH CAROL CHRISTINE, CECILIA ESPINOSA, & JULIA FOURNIER

Acting Out! Combating Homophobia Through Teacher Activism
MOLLIE V. BLACKBURN, CAROLINE T. CLARK, LAUREN M. KENNEY, & JILL M. SMITH, EDS.

Puzzling Moments, Teachable Moments:
Practicing Teacher Research in Urban Classrooms
CYNTHIA BALLENGER

Inquiry as Stance:
Practitioner Research for the Next Generation
MARILYN COCHRAN-SMITH & SUSAN L. LYTLE

Building Racial and Cultural Competence in the Classroom: Strategies from Urban Educators
KAREN MANHEIM TEEL & JENNIFER OBIDAH, EDS.

*(continued)*

PRACTITIONER INQUIRY SERIES, *continued*

Re-Reading Families: The Literate Lives of Urban Children, Four Years Later
CATHERINE COMPTON-LILLY

"What About Rose?" Using Teacher Research to Reverse School Failure
SMOKEY WILSON

Immigrant Students and Literacy
GERALD CAMPANO

Going Public with Our Teaching
THOMAS HATCH ET AL., EDS.

Teaching as Inquiry
ALEXANDRA WEINBAUM ET AL.

"Is This English?" Race, Language, and Culture in the Classroom
BOB FECHO

Teacher Research for Better Schools
MARIAN M. MOHR ET AL.

Imagination and Literacy
KAREN GALLAS

Regarding Children's Words
BROOKLINE TEACHER RESEARCHER SEMINAR

Rural Voices
ROBERT E. BROOKE, ED.

Teaching Through the Storm
KAREN HALE HANKINS

Reading Families
CATHERINE COMPTON-LILLY

Narrative Inquiry in Practice
NONA LYONS & VICKI KUBLER LaBOSKEY, EDS.

Starting Strong
PATRICIA F. CARINI

Because of the Kids
JENNIFER E. OBIDAH & KAREN MANHEIM TEEL

Ethical Issues in Practitioner Research
JANE ZENI, ED.

Action, Talk, and Text
GORDON WELLS, ED.

Teaching Mathematics to the New Standards
RUTH M. HEATON

Teacher Narrative as Critical Inquiry
JOY S. RITCHIE & DAVID E. WILSON

From Another Angle
MARGARET HIMLEY WITH PATRICIA F. CARINI, EDS.

Inside City Schools
SARAH WARSHAUER FREEDMAN ET AL.

Class Actions
JOBETH ALLEN, ED.

Teacher/Mentor
PEG GRAHAM ET AL., EDS.

Teaching Other People's Children
CYNTHIA BALLENGER

Teaching, Multimedia, and Mathematics
MAGDALENE LAMPERT & DEBORAH LOEWENBERG BALL

John Dewey and the Challenge of Classroom Practice
STEPHEN M. FISHMAN & LUCILLE McCARTHY

"Sometimes I Can Be Anything"
KAREN GALLAS

Learning in Small Moments
DANIEL R. MEIER

# Democratic Habits in the Art Classroom

## Supporting Student Voice, Choice, and Community

EDITED BY

Elizabeth Sutton

**TEACHERS COLLEGE PRESS**
**TEACHERS COLLEGE** | COLUMBIA UNIVERSITY
NEW YORK AND LONDON

Published by Teachers College Press,® 1234 Amsterdam Avenue, New York, NY 10027

Copyright © 2024 by Teachers College, Columbia University

Front cover by Rebecca Lown Design. Photo of fourth-grade mosaic by Michelle Cox.

All rights reserved. No part of this publication may be reproduced or transmitted in any form or by any means, electronic or mechanical, including photocopy, or any information storage and retrieval system, without permission from the publisher. For reprint permission and other subsidiary rights requests, please contact Teachers College Press, Rights Dept.: tcpressrights@tc.columbia.edu

*Library of Congress Cataloging-in-Publication Data*

Names: Sutton, Elizabeth A., editor.
Title: Democratic habits in the art classroom : supporting student voice, choice, and community / edited by Elizabeth Sutton.
Description: New York : Teachers College Press, [2023] | Series: Practitioner inquiry series | Includes bibliographical references and index.
Identifiers: LCCN 2023023014 (print) | LCCN 2023023015 (ebook) | ISBN 9780807769003 (paper : acid-free paper) | ISBN 9780807769010 (hardcover : acid-free paper) | ISBN 9780807782040 (ebook)
Subjects: LCSH: Art—Study and teaching--Political aspects. | Democracy—Study and teaching. | Art in education. | Education—Political aspects.
Classification: LCC N350 .D45 2023 (print) | LCC N350 (ebook) | DDC 700.71—dc23/eng/20230816
LC record available at https://lccn.loc.gov/2023023014
LC ebook record available at https://lccn.loc.gov/2023023015

ISBN 978-0-8077-6900-3 (paper)
ISBN 978-0-8077-6901-0 (hardcover)
ISBN 978-0-8077-8204-0 (ebook)

Printed on acid-free paper
Manufactured in the United States of America

# Contents

Acknowledgments     vii

Introduction: Actualizing the Promise     1

**PART I. DEVELOPING CHOICE-BASED CLASSROOMS**     9
*Samantha Goss*

1. Including All Voices in Learning: Peer-to-Peer Verbal Conversations in the Elementary Art Classroom     13
   *Elizabeth S. Bloomburg*

2. Using Meaningful Themes to Guide a Choice-Based Approach to Art Education     26
   *Sandra C. Nyberg*

3. Learning Choices: Students in a Flipped Art Room     44
   *Kathryn Christensen*

**PART II. NURTURING SELF-EFFICACY AND VOICE**     63
*Samantha Goss*

4. How Art Journaling and Studio Habits of Mind Encourage Personal Connections in High School Student Art Making     67
   *Heather Walker*

5. Enhancing Elementary Student Voice Through Art and Advocacy     85
   *Maddison O. Maddock*

6. Self-Efficacy: Empowering Young Artists     99
   *Jodi Fenton*

**PART III. BUILDING COMMUNITIES THAT CARE**     **109**
*Samantha Goss*

7. Art to the Rescue: Exploring Arts-Based Service Learning     113
   *Ashley M. Cardamone*

8. Cultivating Connection Through Community Art     127
   *Lauren Roush*

9. Collaborative Art Making Between 4th-Graders and Community Partners: Its Impact on School Culture     139
   *Michelle Cox*

10. Networks for Building and Supporting Art Education     150
    *Wendy Miller*

Afterword. Defending the Useless: A Neighborhood in Flux     161
*Jeff Rufus Byrd*

Index     171

About the Editor and the Contributors     175

# Acknowledgments

It seems to me that everyone listed in the Contents should be thanked, along with the students and parents who generously gave their creativity, time, and permission. I am so humbled by watching learners grow. Would that we all are lifelong learners, constantly curious! If we teach, we're learning, and as these essays make clear, often the most profound shifts in insight come from careful observation of our students and landscape, integrated with our own experience and knowledge. Professors (experts?) don't hold the only legitimate voices in knowledge-making—this volume demonstrates that knowledge-making is a collaboration of students, teachers, graduate student-teachers, and professors in higher education.

Thank you to Jeff, Wendy, and Samantha. It is the greatest privilege to call my colleagues friends.

Thank you to all the graduate students—those published here, and those who have helped us grow as teachers. You undoubtedly enact a little bit more democracy in your art classes every day.

Thank you for these opportunities for dialogue that make us all grow. As Marit Dewhurst wrote in 2018, "Art both asks the question and tries to answer it: Who are we (and will we be) to each other?" I hope these essays provide a little insight into who we are, and a little hope into who we can be to each other.

# Democratic Habits in the Art Classroom

# Introduction
## Actualizing the Promise

*Elizabeth Sutton*

Since 2016, pundits, politicians, and citizens across the globe have declared that democracy is in crisis. In 2021 Doug Blandy, in his commentary, "Promising Democracy," summarized various precipitating factors of the crisis: the economic and political fallout of the COVID-19 pandemic, including widespread misinformation and xenophobia; the protests responding to the deaths of Black Americans killed by police and general violence against people of color; the January 6, 2021 event of mostly white Trump supporters storming the U.S. Capitol; and the continuing rise of autocratic and authoritarian regimes around the world. As Blandy notes, citizens' existence in a monitory democracy "requires that the public scrutinize decision making and decision makers at all levels within local, state, and national government, as well as nongovernmental organizations, professional associations, advocacy organizations, public interest groups, and nonprofits, among others." (p. 288) To that end, American public education has long emphasized critical thinking and communication skills as core outcomes for students. Our university-level outcomes include critical thinking and oral, written, and visual communication, in addition to depth of knowledge of one's major content area. But is American public education moving away from the creation of a critically thinking, liberally educated citizen also because these skills are necessary for the maintenance of democracy?

Today, these goals and virtues do not seem to be universally held by all Americans. Most Americans believe in a right to education yet do not seem to be able to agree on what education should look like. Public education—and the role of arts in public education—has been assaulted by politicians and legislators seeking to limit teacher and student voice and choice through various cynical and even fascist legislation. In the state of Iowa where my colleagues and I teach preservice art educators and master's candidates in art education, HF 802 (March 16, 2021) is an example of a "divisive concepts" law, restricting what can be taught in classrooms, especially regarding race and racism. In 2023, legislatures in Republican-led states have included gender and sexuality in their drive to limit what concepts can be acknowledged in K–12 schools, following the example set by Florida's so-called "Don't Say Gay" law. Florida's "Parental Rights in Education Act," HB 1557 & SB 1834, has been echoed in bills signed into law in Iowa, including SF 496 and SSB 1197 and proposed or passed in other state legislatures in 2023, including, but not limited to, Indiana, Missouri, New Hampshire, North Dakota, South Carolina, and Tennessee. Iowa has also seen steady declines in funding to both public PK–12 education and higher education—at the same time the ideas of "choice" and "voice" are given as rationale to divert public monies to fund private and charter schools.

As for the arts in public education, they typically are the last to be added to the general curriculum, and the first to go. Perhaps this is because consciously or not, those who dismiss the arts know that art is transformative. As Beverly Naidus makes clear in her book *Arts for Change: Teaching Outside the Frame* (2009), art can serve as a deconstructive force, a prompt to analyze and question what exists and existed, while also being constructive in its ability to visualize that which may be (p. xi). Art education encapsulates the skills purported by universities that they want students to have. Moreover, it creates a space of possibility to imagine and create something entirely new. Art education is also an arena for love and care, as Marit Dewhurst (2022) has discussed. Care ethicists such as Carol Gilligan, Donna Haraway, and Nel Noddings, among others, know that to be in relation is to resist patriarchy, to resist oppression; to be in relation is to be heard.

We will see in the following chapters of this book how students in art education classrooms have been given opportunities to choose, to take control of their own education, to be in relation via their art making. There are too many students in today's schools who go through their days having every choice made for them. They are not given the opportunity to learn what works for them, how to discern, how to reflect, and how to own a path of their making. We will see how art literally is a medium—it helps students access their voices, while developing their critical and relational skills in the process of making art.

Democracy is founded on the belief that citizens have a voice in how they are governed. Obviously, how democracies are structured have provided varying degrees of voice to varying definitions of who constitutes "citizens." If we take as our premise that all human beings, including children, deserve a voice and choice in how they are governed—that self-determination is a fundamental human right—then drawing a parallel between the classroom and society is illustrative. Furthermore, the analogy is potentially transformative. Standing on the shoulders of the giants of philosopher-art educators John Dewey, Maxine Greene, Nel Noddings, bell hooks, and Olivia Gude, the contributors to this volume seek to provide applicable, real-world examples of transformative teaching through giving students voice, choice, and opportunities to care for community. Those three elements are critical to self-efficacy and the development of citizens able to determine their place in the world. As one of the contributors to this volume, Kathryn Christensen, realized, "The art room is an active environment; one with loud thoughts, struggles, and successes. As art teachers, we can strive to teach our students ownership and empowerment through problem-solving, independence, and responsibility within this chaotic yet productive environment" (Chapter 3). Art encourages expression; it encourages discussion; it encourages empathy.

The collection of essays in this book is based on the action research of practicing art educators. As master of arts candidates at the University of Northern Iowa, the contributors of Chapters 1–9 designed, implemented, and synthesized ideas they had as art teachers in the field. While all the contributors are art educators in the Midwest, their classrooms range from elementary to high school, rural to urban. They are from three different cohorts spanning 2015–2021, and some even conducted their research during the first pandemic year of 2020–2021. They are all women, and some are mothers. Given that most art educators are women, that what women do is often seen as less important, even disregarded (hooks, 1994), and that women typically sacrifice their careers first, those of us who mentored these women purposely seek to elevate these professionals' research.

Each of the contributors began thinking about her art class "problem" in my course on curriculum and pedagogy, taken during the first semester in the master's program. From there, they continued to build their familiarity with the scholarly literature and design a research plan. They collected qualitative data in the context of their daily teaching as action research. Their findings and reflections provide an in-depth view into what it is like to be an art teacher in the Midwest today. More important, each chapter presents real-world examples for how to cultivate not only art skills, but the habits of being and interacting that allow humans to contribute meaningfully to this world.

A classroom is a microsociety. Many classrooms are run by teachers who hold their power (and fear) closely, focusing on their own goals, rather than the goals of the students. "Good" students are able to complete projects that look similar at the end—a research paper, a still life painting. "Bad" students might misbehave, do not complete the project, or fail because they did it incorrectly. I was—and to a certain degree, still am—such a teacher, and I still joke about my little dictatorship and my comfort in maintaining a fascist classroom where I get to decide all things. I have been teaching since 2002, and teaching college-age students since 2003. While building a class community has always been important to me, it took me years to grow more comfortable with my skill as a mentor and facilitator of learning, rather than see myself as an authority of knowledge who must maintain control. bell hooks (1994) similarly recognizes how progressives can unwittingly reconstruct oppressive dynamics if the reality of experience and knowledge is not honored. Engaged learning is about hearing others' experiences and witnessing individual expertise in creating a classroom that is a communal space. Once I settled into my identity as mentor and facilitator, my classroom dynamics shifted. I became more intentional with my assignments, thinking about how they functioned, how I could help students relate their lives to content, rather than just trying to make them fun (and not awful to grade). My learning outcomes did not change much, but everyone had more fun, and I had more students engage with me, and with the content. bell hooks (1994) asserts that excitement, passion, and lack of boredom are necessary conditions for engaged learning. When such spaces of relation are created by students and teachers who learn together, the classroom can indeed be "the most radical space of possibility" (p. 12).

I have always felt an uneasy dynamic between creativity/freedom and control, and yet, art and art history drew me in because they resonated with my strong will to be free. For me, it was clear that art and its history are inherently interdisciplinary, that I could use art to teach whatever I wanted—which was, at root, how to be human and engage meaningfully with other humans. I saw art as free from the hindrances of state tests, and in a college setting, I was even more free to teach what I wanted. I may have been uncertain in my pedagogy, but because of my desire to actualize students' own sense of self and being in/with the world, I honored their abilities to create and be free themselves. Indeed, structuring course objectives according to Bloom's Taxonomy of "synthesis" and "creation" is perhaps quaint or simplistic when done superficially, but as so many have pointed out before me, the arts fundamentally synthesize the world around us and co-create new meaning with it and viewers, creating something new all the time. The process of this potential is exciting and meaningful, and co-creation allows for student autonomy, choice, voice, and self-efficacy.

Andratesha Fritzgerald (2020) has provided a cogent explanation of how to honor the learning process and honor students through Universal Design, rather than using a model of central authority and power, which relegates many of the multiplicities of student experiences to the margins. Her design approach is fundamentally culturally sustaining, antiracist, and horizontal; rhizomatic, in postmodern theoretical terms. So too, Shane Safir and Jamila Dugan (2021) show how "street data," or the knowledge from and about students, their families, and community members, can invigorate and engage students and families, as well as teachers and communities. Democratic teaching and learning is necessarily inclusive. I can model and teach *how* to be active, engaged, critically responsive, and socially conscious citizens by how I structure my classroom and assignments and by how and to whom I listen; in other words, by continuously reflecting and improving upon my pedagogy and curriculum in dialogue with others. This is what the contributors in this book have done, and what we share with readers.

## OVERVIEW OF THIS BOOK

The chapters in this book are grouped into three parts that correspond to the habits of being these teacher-contributors chose to focus on: choice, voice, and caring for community. The chapters in each part are introduced by Samantha Goss, a faculty member in the graduate art education program.

In Part I, the three chapters highlight the development of choice-based classrooms. In Chapter 1, Elizabeth Bloomburg, a teacher in an urban school, studied how a flexible art classroom structure at the elementary level (3rd grade) provides opportunities for spontaneous peer collaborations. How themes can function to guide student choices provides the focus for the case study in Chapter 2. Sandra Nyberg's research of 1st- through 5th-grade students in rural school art classes explores the impact of incorporating the meaningful themes of personal identity and community to move to a student-directed curriculum. By way of transition, Chapter 3 is a study of "flipped" instruction as a mechanism to achieve student choice, voice, and self-efficacy with 8th-grade students in a suburban school. Kathryn Christensen shows how flipped instruction provides an opportunity to reach a variety of learners who may struggle with academic, behavioral, and social emotional issues.

The three chapters in Part II emphasize nurturing self-efficacy and voice in students. The impact of art journaling, art making, and Studio Habits of Mind on student motivation and students' personal connections to their art is the focus of Chapter 4. Heather Walker, a high school art teacher in a suburban setting, implemented several teaching strategies and technologies to achieve positive effects. In Chapter 5, Maddison Maddock explores how student voice and efficacy, manifested through the development of communication and leadership skills, can be enhanced through the visual arts. She examines the effects of student-led advocacy experiences on the development of voice in 5th-grade art students in a suburban school, who conceptualized, planned, and hosted a community art-making event with the goal of advocating for the arts. Chapter 6 focuses on understanding the significance of self-efficacy and how it affects students' perseverance and effort in art making. In two urban 5th-grade art classes, Jodi Fenton found that student choice in art making and reflecting processes positively affected their self-efficacy.

The third part of this book is devoted to how to create community: whether that is narrowly defined, as in the art classroom community, or more broadly, as in the case of town–school engagement or taking action on issues that affect all people. In Chapter 7, Ashley Cardamone, a suburban art teacher, uses an arts-based, service-learning project to teach 9th-grade students about animal welfare, specifically the way it was addressed in their own community. Findings from student work samples, written reflections, and teacher observations indicated growth in students' empathy and motivation to take action through creative means in the future. Chapter 8 examines how community art promotes care, connection, and democratic engagement when students build community in their classroom and have a project for the wider community—their town. Lauren Roush describes how her elementary students in 3rd- and 4th-grade art classes designed and installed a collaborative mural in their local library in a rural community. In Chapter 9, collaboration between the art class and the wider school community is shown to be key to building positive school culture. In Michelle Cox's case study, 4th-grade participants in an urban school promoted art education at their school by making a mosaic with parents and teachers. Moving from these intimate, small-scale case studies, Chapter 10 asks readers to zoom out and see how networks between students, teachers, and their communities develop and grow rhizomatically. Faculty member Wendy Miller tells her story of building community with undergraduates and graduates across the state, and how she has maintained and grown a network of actively engaged art educators.

Finally, the Afterword asks readers to see perseverance as a connective habit between art, teaching, learning, and democracy. Jeff Byrd, a faculty member and performance artist, reminds us to keep doing things that don't seem to have value because that is exactly what we need to do to become reflective artists, practitioners, citizens, and beings in the world.

## REFLECTING ON THE PROMISE: ART AND FREEDOM

There is freedom in the art classroom that does not exist in other disciplines. The standards we share are not tested or tied to federal funding; they are not generally the cause for contentious debates about job preparedness or how we fare academically against other nations. Most art teachers are free to develop the pedagogies and content that best serves their students, even in collaboration with their students. We are free to develop the critical thinking, reflecting, and dialogic skills that make democracy. We do so in the *process* of creating, in making something new.

As described in this book, students learn how to deal with process—by making their own decisions, they make meaning; by collaborating with others, they come to recognize meaning is not fixed; by talking together with peers and mentors to reflect on their decision making, they learn not only self-efficacy, but also practice self, peer, and teacher monitoring, creating a mini-democracy in the classroom. Olivia Gude pointed out in her 2009 essay, "Art Education for Democratic Life," that self-awareness and a strong sense of agency are necessary to resist totalitarian ideologies and be civically engaged—to participate in a diverse, complex society. Individuals have to believe that "what we do affects the world around us, that what we do makes a difference" (n.p.). Channeling the existentialist philosopher

Jean-Paul Sartre, Maxine Greene (1988) notes how art education allows each of us to both express the varieties of our internal experiences, as well as perceive the diversity of others' experiences. Art literally provides a medium through existential anxiety—a lens toward the relationality and interconnectedness of beings. We can then choose to be responsible for ourselves, and to care for others. She writes:

> The point is not that there are never any excuses; it is that, in classrooms as well as in the open world, accommodations come too easily. It is the case, as Sartre said, that there is an "anguish" linked to action on one's freedom, and anguish due to the recognition of one's own responsibility for what is happening. The person who chooses himself/herself in his/her freedom cannot place the onus on outside forces. . . . [I]t is his/her interpretation or reading of the situation that discloses possibility; and yet there is no guarantee that the interpretation is correct. (p. 5)

Gude (2009) also understands that meaning-making is not only the purview of art, and that art facilitates its expansion into making meaning with others: It is that "most significantly, engagement with the arts teaches youth to perceive complexity as pleasure and possibility, not as irritating uncertainty. Heightened self-awareness is extended to heightened awareness of others" (n.p.). Building self-efficacy builds resilience, an ability to deal with anxiety and the unknown, *because* we know life is art—both are journeys with no fixed meaning. In life, as in art, "each autonomous individual, with his or her own capacity for seeing and for shaping, must be able to tolerate a sense of aloneness and isolation." In this way, art, and art educators, "help to create the conditions through which individuals experience the pleasures, anxieties, and responsibilities of democratic life" (n.p.).

We are free to make choices. We are free to question. To speak. To challenge. To ask for help. To share with others our experiences. We are free because we have this process of becoming open to us. We are free "not because of what we statically are, but in so far as we are becoming different from what we have been" (John Dewey quoted in Greene, 1988, p. 3).

Art and art education are necessary for democracy now more than ever because art still can be a place of imagining and creating new worlds. John Dewey (2011/1939), on the eve of World War II, in the throes of totalitarian ascendency around the globe, wrote that "democracy is belief in the ability of human experience to generate the aims and methods by which further experience will grow in ordered richness. . . . Since the process of experience is capable of being educative, faith in democracy is all one with faith in experience and education" (p. 151.) Faith in democracy is the belief in human ability to construct rather than destroy. The art classroom—more than any other—can be a proving ground.

## REFERENCES

Blandy, D. (2021). Commentary: Promising democracy. *Studies in Art Education, 62*(3), 286–290. https://doi.org/10.1080/00393541.2021.1936429

Dewey, J. (2011). Creative democracy—The task before us. In Robert B. Talisse & Scott F. Aikin (Eds.), *The pragmatism reader* (pp. 150–154). Princeton University Press. (Original work published 1939)

Dewhurst, M. (2022). Getting ready to relate: Centering radical love in art teacher education. *Art Education, 75*(1), 8–13. https://doi.org/10.1080/00043125.2021.1984799

Fritzgerald, A. (2020). *Antiracism and universal design for learning: Building expressways to success.* CAST.

Greene, M. (1988). *The dialectic of freedom.* Teachers College Press.

Gude, O. (2009). The 2009 Lowenfeld Lecture: Art education for democratic life. *Art Education, 62*(6), 6–11. https://doi.org/10.1080/00043125.2009.11519039

hooks, b. (1994). *Teaching to transgress.* Routledge.

Iowa Legislature. (2021). HF 802. An act providing for requirements related to racism or sexism trainings at, and diversity and inclusion efforts by governmental agencies and entities, s school districts, and public postsecondary educational institutions. https://www.legis.iowa.gov/docs/publications/LGR/89/HF802.pdf

Naidus, B. (2009). *Arts for change: Teaching outside the frame.* New Village Press.

Safir, S., & Dugan, J. (2021). *Street data: A next-generation model for equity, pedagogy, and school transformation.* Corwin.

# Part I

# DEVELOPING CHOICE-BASED CLASSROOMS

*Samantha Goss*

Choice, which is the focus of the next three chapters, allows art educators to "create citizens of a democratic society . . . by creating conditions through which youth experience the pleasure, anxieties, and responsibilities of democratic life" (Gude, 2009, p. 8). The ability to choose and react to the implications of our choices needs to be guided, or taught, in order for each individual to utilize the full potential of their freedom of choice. Dewey (1916) spoke of educational institutions' responsibility "to develop a 'habit of mind'" (p. 99) that would support democratic engagement and choice. Despite Dewey's insistence over 100 years ago, the reality of teaching or even allowing choice in schools has undoubtedly ebbed and flowed depending on multiple layers of context. Gates (2016) points out that student choice in education is not common practice in our schools, and students would likely need significant support if they transitioned to more democratic schools offering choice. By not teaching students how to make choices, educators may contribute to concerns that the general population does not have the knowledge or skills to successfully participate in a democracy (Bolin, 2017). The complexity of implementation is a challenge worth confronting when there are multiple opportunities to make progress in developing the habits of mind necessary for democratic students and citizens.

Art educators, when implementing choice, must first consider their own perspective and positionality in the classroom to ensure a more decentralized classroom to support student choice and co-construction of knowledge (Freire, 2004; Gates, 2016; May, 2011; Stewart & Walker, 2005). When the teacher is no longer in an authoritarian position, other sources of knowledge and learning possibilities can be considered in the curriculum. This shift in perspective is critical for selecting the most beneficial and appropriate places to make student choice the main learning goal. Art content and meaning can become more democratic, as well as the overall frameworks and purposes of art education. Freedman (2000) argued that art in education must be taught and viewed "as a social statement, in a social context, from a social perspective" (p. 326). Her visual-culture approach welcomes and values a multiplicity of context-based visuals as well as student choices on which to critically explore. This not only supports democratic ideals but diversifies art content, promotes criticality, and develops student agency. Big ideas and themes in postmodern art and contemporary art lessons, which complement outcomes of visual culture, support student-driven art exploration and meaning (Gates, 2016). Students must make choices about the conceptual and technical aspects of their art, as the open-ended questions used with big ideas and themes do not have one right answer or even one path to follow. Heise (2013) encourages an empowerment model for arts education that seeks to increase student empowerment through choice, which also builds important life skills. The importance of inclusion, criticality, and prioritizing student perspective in both art content and meaningful lessons reflects opportunities for student choice and empowerment that support a larger goal of creating democratic citizens.

In Chapter 1, the research of Elizabeth Bloomburg reflects the importance of student choice in developing democratic citizens. Students showed the ability to have a common goal while making choices about their individual roles and actions. Students demonstrated awareness of their strengths and their ability to decide how and when to use them (Moffett, 1998). Some chose to work together or not to varying degrees and with compromise; decisions that they will undoubtedly navigate countless times in their lives that support the respect for individuals and the shared goals of democracy. Additionally, the students were innovative and open to change, which echoes Dewey's (1916) explanation that education should not maintain current societal norms alone but prepare democratic citizens to imagine and enact change.

Sandra Nyberg, in Chapter 2, provides another opportunity to consider how art education balances teaching established norms while being open to change. A focus on technical art learning reinforces important norms but can be limiting when that is the scope of a lesson. She shifted her focus to help students drive the why of their lessons through exploration and choice in order to increase ownership and investment. The teacher created a space for change through choice and remained open to how students would contribute to that transformation. Providing choice can enhance intrinsic motivation for students (Gates, 2016), encouraging them to practice being change-makers. At the end of Nyberg's research, over half the students felt they could make choices and express themselves most of the time. It is important to teach students how their choices use knowledge of existing norms and their own motivations for change in the context of art making and as a member of a democratic society whether it be in the art classroom or beyond.

Finally, in Chapter 3, Kathryn Christensen considers how the flipped-classroom model develops student choice and independence. Students were able to choose their own learning paths, which required them to consider their own strengths and needs when selecting paths and possibilities in the art lesson. This self-awareness and dedication to their own capabilities connect to Dewey's desire for habits of mind to allow for personal capability development and the ability to apply these skills meaningfully in society (Meadows, 2019). This circles back to Bloomburg's research in Chapter 1 where students considered themselves and their choices as individuals and members of a group with a common goal. Nyberg's research in Chapter 2 also conveys the importance of preparing students to feel empowered to make choices. Student empowerment and the ability to see their role in a larger group informs the choices that prepare students to make change democratically in their artwork, classroom, and future society.

## REFERENCES

Bolin, T. D. (2017). Struggling for democracy: Paulo Freire and transforming society through education. *Policy Futures in Education, 15*(6), 744–766.

Dewey, J. (1916). *Democracy and education: A introduction to the philosophy of education*. The Free Press.

Freedman, K. (2000). Social perspectives on art education in the U.S.: Teaching visual culture in a democracy. *Studies in Art Education, 41*(4), 314–329.

Freire, P. (2004). *Pedagogy of the oppressed*. Continuum.

Gates, L. (2016). Rethinking art education practice one choice at a time. *Art Education, 69*(2), 14–19.

Gude, O. (2009). The 2009 Lowenfeld Lecture: Art education for democratic life. *Studies in Art Education, 62*(6), 6–11.

Heise, D. (2013). Fostering resiliency through the arts. In K. Tavin & C. B. Morris (Eds.), *Stand(ing) up for a change: Voices of arts educators* (pp. 112–120). National Art Education Association.

May, H. (2011). Shifting the curriculum: Decentralization in the art education experience. *Art Education, 64*(3), 33–41.

Meadows, E. (2019). What is a democracy? What does education in a democracy need to be according to Dewey? In C. L. Lowery & P. N. Jenlink (Eds.), *The handbook of Dewey's educational theory and practice* (pp. 21–40). Brill.

Moffett, J. (1998). *The universal schoolhouse: Spiritual awakening through education.* Calendar Island Publishers.

Stewart, M., & Walker, S. (2005). *Rethinking curriculum in art.* Davis.

# CHAPTER 1

# Including All Voices in Learning
## Peer-to-Peer Verbal Conversations in the Elementary Art Classroom

*Elizabeth S. Bloomburg*

Imagine walking into an elementary art classroom: There is a buzz and the excitement of tiny hands at work. Sounds of students laughing and conversing fill the space, while the teacher is busy encouraging a struggling student. Then *that* moment comes: The teacher wonders if the volume of laughter and small voices is getting a little too loud or the class is laughing a little bit too much, which prompts her to remind the class of table work expectations. Are the students really off task, or is the teacher assuming they are? Are they on task but too loud to promote a successful learning environment? How can students benefit from talking together, and how can educators influence discussions to further learning? How can teachers effectively build students' empathy for one another through dialogue? Who should dominate conversations in the classroom during instruction and work time?

The basis for this study is my reflection on a similar moment that occurred in my classroom a few years ago. Fourth-grade students were working in groups to create a collaborative architectural sculpture. Moments later, their general classroom teacher walked into the art room and exclaimed: "Class, remember we are working on whisper-level voice in group work. This is way too loud!" The teacher then proceeded to go around the room to show each group the hand signal for quiet voices. It is not typical that a classroom teacher would try to manage the art room, and I was taken aback at this moment. Although it was done with good intentions, it led me to rethink how the school environment and culture can stifle students' creative thinking and dialogue. Can these restrictive expectations limit our students? Does creative, collaborative, dialogic group work give classroom teachers, administration, or even parents the impression students are not focused, working, or engaged?

My classroom research furthered my understanding of how peer-to-peer conversations contribute to authentic art making and demonstrate how teachers can foster peer conversations to aid students in authentic art making through real-world application in elementary art lessons. I wanted to provide teachers with better insight into how a flexible classroom structure provides opportunities for spontaneous peer collaborations. I wondered:

- How can student-to-student conversations contribute to authentic art making?
- How can students develop empathy through art making and dialogue?
- What do elementary students record about the process of collaborating when the teacher is not there?
- How do students revise their work based on peer feedback?

In creative teaching and learning, students have an opportunity to experiment, interact, and participate in the collaborative construction of their own knowledge and learn higher-order thinking skills. In such an open-ended classroom, all participants co-construct equally during the flow of conversation. Learning takes place as a group effort, and learning cannot be scripted because the students must have an active role in constructing the conversation together. Improvisational teaching has a structure that is flexible and planned by the teacher, but it is open-ended and allows for a give and take by the group. The teacher must manage a balance between the structure and the improvisation through setting flexible routines, which is a learned skill.

Conversation helps build these skills. Teachers can provide the space for conversation and dialogic learning. With respect to art, Szekely (1982) discussed why it is important to talk to children about art, what to discuss, and when to discuss it. These conversations help students to visualize and plan what they are about to create. Huard (2017) suggests that some art teachers put off discussing artwork with young students, pointing out that they perceive there to be not enough time. Teachers want students to have as much time to make art as possible at the cost of discussions. Huard encourages teachers to facilitate focused discussions on a consistent basis, in the interest of making each minute more effective when these discussions become part of daily art making. She states that as educators, we make the decision to have meaningful conversations with students. She echoes Szekely by stating if we do not make a habit of talking about art with students, it will not happen. Huard goes on to explain that her curriculum intentionally delves into all cultures, giving each culture equal weight and time; nothing is tacked on in the end. She points out that conversations with students should be the same, that conversations should continue from class to class, and that discussions are not a box to tick off from a list. She refers to Olivia Gude's teaching on open-ended projects, which are designed to open to unexpected possibilities for students. The challenge lies in planning and research for the teacher, managing the discussion, and having the courage to discuss uncomfortable topics. Huard says if a conversation becomes controversial, and the teacher shies away, it is all right for the curriculum to circle back around and discuss the topic again. She admits some conversations might become awkward, but the more the teacher practices, the more familiar uncomfortable conversations will become to the teacher and students. Giving students the time and space for conversation gives them the opportunity to bring deeper meaning to their creative work and increase their engagement in their work and the class.

When students engage in authentic dialogue, they become active participants in learning by making connections between themselves and the rest of the world within a caring community. Phillips (2003) elaborates on the significance of empathetic teaching practices by offering a window into the school where she teaches, which values and models an atmosphere of caring and respect for students. Caring, according to Noddings (2012), is an act of engagement with other people. It is an action, not a trait, which is taught through example and requires engagement. Noddings teaches that modeling and dialogue are necessary for teachers to teach empathy. Teachers use positive motivation to encourage students to become inquiry-based learners. Teachers model for students how much they care through their actions. Students whose voices are valued speak up and are willing participants in their own learning. At the same time, students learn to value what others have to say and listen to multiple viewpoints when the teacher models this for them.

Thus teachers play an important role in creating an empathetic and caring environment, and when students engage in dialogue, they build communication and higher-order thinking skills in the elementary art room. The kind of feedback a teacher gives students can affect the frequency and quality of peer conversation and learning. Teachers will see a benefit to their students when discussions are a habit and it has been established that all students can learn from one another and have a say.

Providing students with the freedom to show others what they know is how educators empower students to own their knowledge and to share and construct knowledge together. Students each experience learning in their own way with their constructed prior knowledge. Every student has a unique set of experiences and interpretation of those experiences. It is essential to give a voice to all students, including those who may be more introverted or are learning a second language. Through conversation and reflection, students think and reconsider the decisions they have made, then they become the artists. Every interaction I have with a student can change what I become and change the person the student becomes. I recognized that a transformative framework applies to this study, as my goal was to include all voices and to create a safe environment, where students are given a voice and learn to listen to one another.

My study was conducted at a suburban public elementary school in Iowa. One of five elementary schools within a growing district, this school has over 720 students ranging from kindergarten to 5th grade. For my research, I focused on one section of 22 3rd-grade students who have art class for 70 minutes once a week. The participants consisted of 11 girls and 11 boys, including 5 English language learners (3 boys and 2 girls), and 1 girl with an individualized education plan (IEP).

I designed lessons to enhance collaboration and group conversations. These included the following pedagogical strategies:

- Students choosing their own seats to create a flexible environment
- Beginning class with 10 minutes of free sketching
- Giving minimal teacher feedback
- Utilizing a think-pair-share teaching strategy in whole group discussions

The unit of the study was based on endangered animals, environmental art, and ecology, and therefore class projects reflected this content. As I will describe in this chapter, my pedagogical strategies facilitated learner interaction to enhance connection and construction of the meaning of this content.

## PAINTING PORTRAITS OF ENDANGERED SPECIES ANIMALS

The focus for the 12-week unit was painting portraits of endangered species animals. As shown in Table 1.1, I used several art projects in the first 6 weeks of the unit to model basic studio skills and class behavior expectations. In Week 7 I introduced the class to the endangered species project by having students explore why animals become endangered. Students watched a video of a local zoo's contributions to animal sanctuaries around the world and discussed with partners the reasons for endangerment. Then the class watched a video from the environmental artist Aurora Robson. Robson's work uses recycled plastic of various colors to create large, abstract sculptures with ecological themes. Students discussed with peers why Robson creates art. During work time, I gave students the choice of where to sit and with whom to work. Students generated ideas using iPads and sketchbooks. Students logged onto the World Wildlife Fund website and explored a variety of endangered species, before selecting a particular animal to paint. They recorded their research in their sketchbooks to consult when creating their final work in the coming days. The research consisted of sketches of their animal, the location of the animal's habitat, and statistics about the animal.

During Week 8, students began class with a quiet free sketchbook time. I gave students time to draw whatever they wanted for the first 10 minutes

**Table 1.1. Description of Progression of Weekly Class Sessions**

| Week | Summary of Class Activities |
|---|---|
| 1 | Group newspaper structures and students choose seats |
| 2 | Create sketchbook covers and staple book together |
| 3 | Get-to-know-you game: 3D paper sculptures of partners |
| 4 | Introduction of illuminated letters |
| 5 | Review using think-pair-share, then work on illuminated letters |
| 6 | Finish illuminated letters and introduce Inktober challenge, closing circle using pair sharing |
| 7 | Introduction to endangered animals project, then watch a video about Aurora Robson and research animals on www.wwf.org on iPads and brainstorm in sketchbooks |
| 8 | Students free draw in a sketchbook first 10 minutes, then watch a PBS video about why we should care about endangered species, learn about the street artist Pejac, sketch out underpainting drawing, and learn about the rule of thirds |
| 9 | Students free draw in a sketchbook first 10 minutes, watch a PBS video about how much plastic is in the oceans, and painting Day 1 |
| 10 | Continue free sketch, introduce the collaborative art of Olly and Suzi and watch Olly and Suzi video of animals' reaction to their artwork, discuss respect for a living creature, and continue painting Day 2 |
| 11 | Continue free sketch, partner-share activity, and continue/finish painting Day 3; a representative from Polk County Conservation speaks to the class about threatened species in the state; postsurvey, and reflection through the title of the artwork |
| 12 | Continue free sketch and finish painting Day 4 |

of the class using only a pencil or pen. Then students explored the concepts of ecosystems through a PBS video about why one should care about endangered species. Next, I introduced the class to street artist Pejac, who works in a variety of media including drawing, painting, collage, sculpture, and videography. His creations center around the theme of the human effect on the world and individual ecosystems, for example, in the Arctic Circle. With partners, students discussed why Pejac creates art and then shared their ideas with the entire class. After that, I introduced the rule of thirds, and the class identified how Pejac uses the rule of thirds to attract attention to his work. I then demonstrated how to create an underpainting drawing on a large scale. Students created their drawing of their chosen animal on an 18" x 24" paper with the assistance of their sketchbook and iPad (Figure 1.1).

**Figure 1.1. Student using an iPad to draw chosen animal**

On the third day of the unit (Week 9), many students asked me if they would be given free draw time in the beginning of class again. One student expressed that he wanted to continue working on his sketch from last week. I responded positively and gave students time to work on whatever they wanted. Afterward, the class gathered on the carpet and watched a PBS video about plastic in the ocean and discussed the impact plastic has on the environment. Students discussed with partners the environment of the animal they had chosen and what they would add to the background of their work to show the story of the animal. I gave a demonstration of how to mix liquid tempera and how to mix the color brown in three different ways to get three different types of brown. Students worked together to gather supplies and choose workspaces; some students even chose to sit under a table, while others chose their table spots (Figure 1.2).

The Week 10 class began with another free drawing session, and students were introduced to the artist collaboration of Olly and Suzi. Their work focuses on the idea of animals being living entities and having a spirit.

**Figure 1.2. Students sharing mixed colors at their chosen seats**

Students were shown a video in which Olly and Suzi create artwork in the animal's environment and then present the work to the animal, including a shark who bites off a large section of the work. Students were then asked to discuss how their work would tell a story about their animal and how it could show the spirit of the animal. Then they continued painting their work.

For the fifth day of the unit (Week 11), I had arranged for a representative from the local County Conservation Board to visit the class. She gave a 45-minute talk about the history of endangered animals within Iowa, with engaging questions for students to answer. Students learned that bobcats were predators that are now extinct in our state due to farmers and cities wanting to keep their land safe. Additionally, they learned river otters almost became extinct in our state because of overhunting. The guest speaker brought two live animals for students to learn about: an ornate boxed turtle and a speckled king snake. In addition, there were a variety of items for students to interact with, including a bobcat pelt, an otter pelt, a bat house, a purse made of snakeskin, and a stuffed barred owl. After the presentation, students completed the paintings they had already begun, with renewed interest and engagement. Providing structure through planned sketches, artist examples, and real-life experiences with animals sparked and maintained student interest.

## FACILITATING DIALOGIC LEARNING

Having reviewed above the chronological presentation of lessons from my unit on painting portraits of endangered animals, in the following sections, I analyze the findings that emerged from my action research.

### Effects of Teacher Actions

Teacher actions can cultivate an empathetic, caring environment. I demonstrated care, created flexible seating chosen by students, limited supplies to increase student interactions, and was careful about feedback, requiring students to work silently during sketchbook times. Students were enthusiastic about choosing their own seats and working where they wanted. They chose a variety of areas throughout the classroom, including under a counter, on the floor, or at tablespaces. Flexible seating led to flexible groupings. For example, Ivan and another student researched animals together on the first day and the next day split up when they decided to create different animals. In contrast, Luke and Katie consistently worked together under a table every day of the endangered animal project. They shared supplies while working on different animals; Luke worked on tigers and Katie worked on sharks.

The results of a survey given to students before and after the project showed a significant increase in students who always or often found it helpful to work with others when making art. Presurveys show a combined 47.8% felt working with others often or always helped, while postsurveys indicated 60.9% felt it often or always helped, demonstrating an overall increase of 13.1%.

\* \* \*

Additionally, I included silent work time with sketchbooks. Although students would ask questions about sharpening pencils or using scented markers, this mostly quiet time in the classroom became a time where students would share problems with me one on one. I built relationships and demonstrated care when students opened up. One student told me about health problems facing a sibling in NICU (Neonatal Intensive Care Unit), while another student informed me about a death in her family. In contrast, two different students found a creative way around the silent rule and began having a written conversation in their sketchbooks about a video game. They told me they were "book talking." I could have redirected their attention or reprimanded them, however, instead I praised their creative thinking and encouraged the pair to draw the video game together. I identified these moments as opportunities to build my relationship with my students, while creating a teachable moment to demonstrate empathy and care for others to the class.

**Development of Peer Relationships**

The theme of peer relationships emerged from field notes, surveys, student interviews, and student artwork. Peer relationships were influenced by the safe and flexible environment cultivated by my actions. In the presurveys, a combined total of 55% of students felt that others always or often listened to their ideas, 10% felt sometimes listened to, and 30% of students felt rarely or never listened to. The postsurveys show the combined percentage of students who felt others always or often listened to their ideas increased to a total of 63.6%, while the percentage of students who felt rarely or never listened to decreased to 27.3%.

During the study, students intuitively formed groups of two or three or worked alone based on what they felt secure with. Some peer relationships were previously established friendships, including Channing and Tyler, who worked together closely on tiger paintings. In an interview, Tyler said he picked a tiger because it was what Channing wanted to make and "tigers are pretty cool." In conversations with each other, Tyler and Channing discussed next steps for their work and it was their goal to make their work as similar as possible to create two copies (Figures 1.3 and 1.4). Other peer relationships were unpredictable and developed during the project. Ella and

**Figure 1.3. Artwork by Channing**

**Figure 1.4. Artwork by Tyler**

Ivan began to work together on the second day of painting. In a field note (2018), I wrote about their conversation with each other:

> Ella said, "We are doing the same animal but totally different strategies." Ivan replied, "That's good that I'm doing this, do not copy me!" This is an unlikely pair—I wouldn't have thought they would want to work together. Once they worked together I could understand why—they are both playful and imaginative students—they worked really well together.

The two worked together from that point on, comparing work and creating a competitive but understanding environment.

Another unlikely pairing echoing that understanding was that of Ava and Damien. During an interview, Damien and Ava both discussed how they were creating turtles together. Ava was quick to point out she was creating a sea turtle because she liked to visit the beach and swim, while Damien chose to create a different type of turtle. On the first day of painting together, Ava mixed the whole paint tray, blending colors she was supposed to share with Damien. He calmly helped her to clean it up at the sink, stating he knew it wasn't on purpose.

## Awareness of Others and the World

Care and empathy towards each other and the world were exhibited by students in a variety of ways. Some students demonstrated empathy for each other during working together, while other students demonstrated care for endangered species and the environment. During the presurvey, 41.6% of students responded with always or often having something to say to help others' work, while the postsurveys showed a combined 69.6%. Postsurveys showed a significant increase of 28% of students who felt they always or often had something to say to help others' work.

One particular group of students worked together after one student, Eddie, struggled with mistakes made in his work. Ivan and Ella worked with Eddie to create a red panda. In a student interview, Ella explained Eddie messed up on his first work and came to Ivan and her for help. Eddie added they were "kinda professionals." Ivan interjected, "Probably because we have experience and my dad is an artist." The group worked together to mix the correct colors and shared the colors. This encounter is an example of students showing empathy for one another as a group.

Other students demonstrated empathy for endangered animals and the environment through their work. Paige connected real-life application in her artwork (Figure 1.5). In a conversation during work time, Paige expressed to me she had seen sea turtles on her family vacation to Florida. She chose to paint a sea turtle for this reason. Paige states in the title of her work, "Sea turtles are endangered, you need to help them by NOT!!! Littering please!!!" She is pleading with the viewer to clean up the environment and avoid littering.

**Figure 1.5. Final work by Paige**

## Preference for Independent Work

The theme of independent work emerged unexpectedly, and I discovered it by analyzing student sketchbook work, student interviews, photos of students working, and student postsurveys. In the presurveys, 43% of students preferred to work with a partner, 35% of students preferred to work alone, and 9% of students preferred to work with a group of people. The postsurveys found the percentage of students who preferred to work alone increased to 48%, while the percentage of students preferring to work with a partner decreased to 39%.

There were a couple of students who worked completely alone throughout the study. Anna was a student who always sat with other students but worked independently the entire time. When interviewed, Anna said she chose a tiger, "because I went on a search and I saw a number of people attacking [tigers] and I wanted to know more information about tigers." Anna consistently worked alone on her idea of a tiger attack for weeks, including mixing her own colors (Figures 1.6–1.8). When asked if she was working with anyone else, she referred to other students also working on tigers and stated "Umm, actually me and Channing are doing a tiger. But I don't know if he's working with anybody." Anna did not refer to working with Channing, only that his work was about the same animal. This interaction is an example of how some students preferred to work independently, while at the same time being aware of what others were doing.

The postsurveys found the percentage of students always or often making changes after peer feedback decreased from 45.5% to 26%, suggesting further development of independence and independent thinking, even while caring about each other's work. Implementing changes after peer feedback was originally a central focus of the study. The focus later shifted to cultivating empathy for one another and endangered animals. In the end, changes

**Figure 1.6. Sketch of a tiger by Anna**

**Figure 1.7. Anna working on a tiger painting**

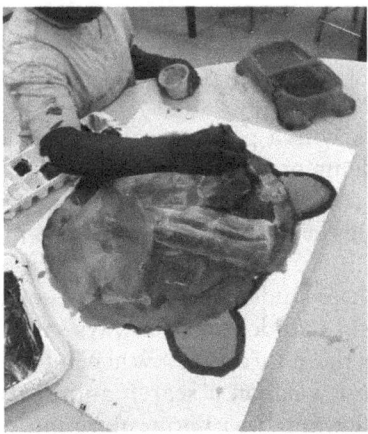

**Figure 1.8. Final tiger artwork by Anna**

to work after feedback was not explicitly taught and further research is required to determine what effect a flexible structure would have.

## CONCLUSIONS

When combined, implementing a flexible classroom structure, pre-content modeling, and skill-based tasks helped to create a safe and empathetic environment for learning. In my classroom, surveys showed that more students felt working with others helped them, more students felt comfortable to talk with others about their work, and a large majority (69.6%) of students felt they had something to say to help others' work.

Currently, there are research examples of discussion and dialogic-teaching practice being used at the secondary level (Kakas, 1991; Loh, 2015; Sedlacek & Sedova, 2017). However, at the elementary level there is inadequate research on how peer-to-peer verbal communication affects learning. This study aimed to provide elementary art teachers with better insight into how a flexible structure provides opportunities for spontaneous peer collaborations.

I began by trying to gain a window into what students discuss while creating art to see if conversations were of value in the learning process. As the study progressed, it became clear that students' conversations transformed into an avenue for creating empathy for one another. At the end of the study, I found that students valued a variety of different workspaces and different ways to work. Some students prefer to work alone at a table while being aware of others, some like to work with one partner on the floor, and others will work with a larger group under a table, or a variety of other combinations. I found that it is important to let students choose where and how they work best and allow them to change their minds or try different approaches to a problem. This flexible structure gives students power and a voice in how they learn and provides them with a safe and empathetic classroom.

## REFERENCES

Huard, M. (2017). The case for class discussion: Sixth-grade's exploration of El Anatsui's contemporary sculpture. *Art Education, 70*(6), 14–19.

Kakas, K. (1991, Autumn). Classroom communication during fifth-grade students' drawing lessons: Student-student and student-teacher conversations. *Studies in Art Education, 33*(1), 21–35.

Loh, V. (2015, September). The power of collaborative dialogue. *Art Education, 68*(5), 14–19.

Noddings, N. (2012). The language of care ethics. *Knowledge Quest, 40*(4), 53–56.

Phillips, L. (2003, June). Nurturing empathy. *Art Education, 56*(4), 45–53.

Sedlacek, M., & Sedova, K. (2017). How many are talking? The role of collectivity in dialogic teaching. *International Journal of Educational Research, 85*, 99–108.

Szekely, G. (1982). Conversations in the art class. *Art Education, 35*(3), 15–17.

CHAPTER 2

# Using Meaningful Themes to Guide a Choice-Based Approach to Art Education

*Sandra C. Nyberg*

The camel hair bristles drooped under the weight of the bright orange watercolor. The young artist carefully touched the tip of his brush to the surface of his damp paper. In an instant the bright orange swirled across the page in a frenzied rush as though it had just escaped confinement . . . running and twirling in an unchoreographed dance of freedom and happiness. Delighted gasps bounced around the art room as students experienced their first introduction to wet-on-wet watercolor technique. First-graders continued to paint the interiors of their oil pastel leaves with a water wash, and then dash and dab with red, magenta, yellow, and gold. I walked around the room, sharing the moment, ooh-ing and ah-ing as they showed me their favorite swirls. It was magical: For them, the paint was magical . . . for me, their reactions were magical.

"Why are we doing this?" a student asked. It struck me. It was a question rarely asked. A classmate sitting nearby chimed in immediately, "To learn about wet-on-wet painting!" Another joined in, "And about hot and . . . I mean, *warm* and cool colors." Then another, "And organic lines and shapes in nature!" Yes. Correct. They all seemed to grasp the objectives and my curious student was satisfied with the "right answers" of his classmates. He continued to dash and dab his own leaf contentedly.

As I walked home that afternoon, the fallen leaves littered my street like confetti; fiery splashes of red and orange against the black pavement. Still, each leaf echoed the innocent question of my equally fiery artist.

*Why are we doing this?*

Even amidst the magic, I knew the given *why* was not enough. Although my artists were content, even delighted, I knew that a watercolor leaf painting was short-changing their creative potential, their authentic voice. Technique and color theory should not be the only *why*.

During this time, I was learning about a new philosophy for teaching art called Teaching for Artistic Behavior (TAB). This choice-based pedagogy values student choice and autonomy, shifting creative control to students and providing a studio-based classroom environment. Under this philosophy, exploration, inquiry, and creativity thrive (Hathaway & Jaquith, 2014).

Even though choice-based pedagogy is not new, the TAB philosophy and community was something new to me. After learning about this innovative approach to art education, I began asking myself: Why am I so apprehensive to try it myself, when deep down I know there is so much more that my artists could be experiencing?

Choice-based art programs, like TAB, provide authentic learning environments that foster creativity, collaboration, and reflection (Hathaway & Jaquith, 2014). Students who are personally invested and authentically engaged in the learning process continue to ask *why*, but are driven by reflection and authentic meaning-making: Why am *I* making this choice? . . . Rather than why are *you* making me do this? As educators, we must ask ourselves this same question with every curricular choice we make. A choice-based approach to art education replaces product-focused curriculum with an emphasis on authentic student choice and discovery (Hathaway & Jaquith, 2014). Students learn that they are capable, creative, and that their voice matters (Arao & Clemens, 2013; Pellish, 2012; Walker, 2004). By instilling these beliefs in our students, we lay a foundation in which students become engaged learners and confident in their abilities to make a difference—to become change-makers (Arao & Clemens, 2013).

However, moving to a choice-based curriculum requires more than simply accepting new ideology. This shift requires art teachers to let go of familiar beloved projects, and at times, parent and district support (Anderson & Milbrandt, 1998; Douglas, 2012; Gude, 2013). As educators, we must be willing to redefine our definitions of success in order to provide our students with what many of us know, deep down, is a more meaningful and authentic art-making experience.

In 2018–2019 I explored how meaningful themes can be fused with a choice-based approach to art education in order to engage 1st- through 5th-grade students within a rural school district. It is my intention to demonstrate the potential impact of transitioning from a teacher-directed, discipline-based curriculum to one of exploration and discovery. I analyzed how meaningful themes, specifically identity and community, support a choice-based curriculum and revised classroom setup. Student choice and personal meaning-making became a catalyst for a more holistic approach to art education; one in which student voice was valued and young artists were empowered to find and use their authentic voices.

Decades of research promote the advantages of a choice-based curriculum in art education. Still, well-meaning and passionate educators continue to cling to teacher-directed styles of classroom management and curriculum, teaching very similarly to how we were taught and what we have seen

(Efland, 1976; Gude, 2013). Although evidence supports student-directed projects, gaps continue to remain in research. My case study provides applicable tools for how using themes as scaffolding during the transition to a choice-based classroom benefits the student's overall art experience.

Making this shift requires educators to embrace ambiguity (Hathaway & Jaquith, 2014) and to step into a process of exploration, discovery, and deep reflection. Art educators must transform their teaching practices, strategies, and philosophies, oftentimes giving up the familiar and redefining what success looks like within the elementary art room.

My intent is to promote and encourage the student-driven *why*. This study explores how the meaningful themes of identity and community can be used to guide students into using their artistic voices to make powerful change, both internally and externally. As educators transform their philosophy and practices, perhaps students will become better equipped to find their authentic voices and to then use their voices for positive change, making this world a better place.

### "LET THEM FLY"

Three years ago my nephew came home from his first day of kindergarten and shared with my sister that his new school was a *good* school, but that his old school was a *great* school, because at his old school *they kept him safe and let him fly*. Upon hearing his story, I etched his simply profound words upon my heart and began a mission to transform my teaching philosophy into one that would match the wisdom of a 5-year-old. "Keep them safe . . . *and* let them fly." My selected vehicle to explore this transformation is through the concomitance of meaningful themes and a choice-based curriculum. The belief that our children can truly be empowered to make the world a better place drives the transformation in curriculum and pedagogy that I would be orchestrating within my classroom.

A transformative framework supports the vision of allowing our young artists to fly by calling for social action. As choice-based art allows students to find their authentic voices, a transformative framework guides the use of their voices as a platform for social action. Although an ideal goal, true equality does not exist in our society. Human values are intrinsically embedded within research. Research studies therefore have the opportunity, the responsibility, to address the human condition (Sweetman et al., 2010).

A transformative framework recognizes the societal realities of power dynamics and marginalization (Creswell, 2013). By recognizing that knowledge is reflected by power and social relationships, we are called to use our cognition to improve society and help others to do the same, protecting and honoring the voices of marginalized populations (Mertens, 2003).

Authentic art instruction occurs when art making is tied to real life and to the actual methodologies of contemporary artists (Anderson & Milbrandt, 1998). In order for schools to prepare students to be successful in life beyond the school walls, art education must confront and incorporate life issues that veritably reflect modern culture. Simultaneously, students must be immersed in strategic idea generation and problem-solving. Anderson and Milbrandt (1998) suggest three strategic goals of authentic art instruction: (1) discipline-centered inquiry, (2) knowledge construction in lieu of passive acceptance, and (3) real-world connection-making (p. 16).

Art educators acknowledge the importance of creativity and process over product. However, breaking free from traditional models of art education, those that perpetuate the school art style, takes decisive and deliberate action. Gude (2013) advocates that we reconsider the way in which art education is currently being taught within our public schools. In response to Efland's (1976) analysis and Anderson and Milbrandt's (1998) reaction, Gude suggests that quality art projects incorporate complex strategies and require investigation and real-life connection. She contends that the influence of the educator has the power to support creativity and meaningful exploration of the content. Art teachers hold power to either encourage or stifle a child's curiosities and creativity; consequently, school art style may not lack authenticity in itself. If school art reflects the values of the institution (Efland, 1976), then what should art educators value when designing an art curriculum? Gude (2013) offers multiple suggestions of worthy values:

- Engaging in authentic artistic processes over making copies
- Utilizing skills, forms, and vocabulary in authentic contexts over de-contextualized exercises and recipes
- Investigating over symbolizing
- Experiencing as much as making

Therefore, school art projects themselves are not the problem. According to Gude, good art projects provide a means by which students are able to construct their own meaning.

Hathaway and Jaquith (2014) promote an alternative solution to combat the predetermined products of mainstream art education. As I mentioned earlier, Teaching for Artistic Behavior is a movement that promotes a choice-based approach to art education: one that promotes autonomy and student decision making. In TAB, educators implement a studio-style classroom setup in which materials, equipment, and resources are organized by media and content into studio centers that authentically mirror workspaces of practicing artists. The studio setup and curriculum support student choice, exploration, and experimentation. Teacher-directed learning is replaced with a choice-based approach, positioning students to become self-directed as they generate and manifest their own ideas. It seems no wonder that TAB has great potential for modeling and supporting creativity and authenticity.

Opportunities for authentic student exploration and choice are becoming endangered, especially within my current school district. Center times have been cut from all schedules, including kindergarten. Teachers are under pressure to adhere to a strict daily schedule of 90 minutes of reading and writing and 60 minutes of math. In order to meet these administrative demands, classroom teachers are unable to provide significant time for authentic student discovery and choice. Jaquith and Hathaway (2012) suggest that by focusing on exploration and discovery within the curriculum and learning environment, "all aspects of teaching and learning are examined through the lens of transformation" (p. 2).

Transformation occurred on multiple levels throughout my study. As the teacher, I reevaluated my role within the classroom, stepped out of a position of control, and stepped into the role of facilitator. Students became equal participants in the research, discovering and exploring beside me. They began the transformation of self-discovery and personal expression. No longer fed the solution or provided with a step-by-step guide, young artists actively explored and created meaning. This process lays the groundwork of their capability (Jaquith, 2012).

Supporting the autonomy of my students sends the clear message that they are capable and that expressing their voice matters. When students learn for themselves that their ideas are valid and important, they potentially gain the confidence needed to take action, discovering for themselves their capability of creating a positive impact.

Teachers have the opportunity to facilitate experiences in which students and teacher together learn to critically examine the social conditions around them. Pairing student-driven choice with teacher facilitation and support can empower young artists to step into the role of change-makers.

When I learned that our district would be cutting centers from the kindergarten curriculum, TAB became more than just intriguing, it became hope. The hope that within the walls of my own space and the confines of my own subject matter, I could begin making choices for my artists that would provide a safe space for them to fly. Gone was my motivation to look good at art shows, to bask in compliments from parents and administrators, and to breeze through my day with reliable and "successful" products. In place of those desires was a need to facilitate authentic student voice.

## TRANSITIONING TO CHOICE

With the impetus of losing kindergarten centers, I decided it was time to make a change. I studied the effects of the transition in my art classroom from a teacher-directed curriculum to a choice-based curriculum in

1st- through 5th-grade students in a Midwestern rural public school. The school serves primarily a middle-class population made up of 91 percent White students, 6 percent Hispanic, and 3 percent other. The district reports that 23% of families qualify for free or reduced lunches.

The objective of my research was to answer the question: How can a choice-based approach to art education be used in conjunction with meaningful themes to increase student engagement and personal connection and meaningfulness? The study included four main components: (1) classroom setup and studio design, (2) classroom procedures and expectations, (3) thematic overview and curriculum design, and (4) student handout and survey creation. In this section I explain how I implemented these components in my classroom, and in the following sections I will analyze my use of the themes of personal identity and community to achieve the goals of my research.

**Studio Centers Offered**

I began my transition towards TAB by first selecting which studio centers to offer. The goal was to provide students with a range of choices and possibilities that would attract varying learning styles and artistic preferences. In addition to student appeal, I also considered function and manageability. Supplies needed to be age-appropriate and resourcefully stocked. I chose seven centers: Architecture (e.g., blocks, Legos); Messy 3D (i.e., modeling clay, papier-mâché); Fibers & Textiles; Painting; Collage; Sculpture (e.g., glue guns, cardboard, found objects); and Drawing & Coloring. In addition to the studio centers, I provided a floor space and demonstration table for mini-lessons and/or reflection and sharing times. These spaces were set up to accommodate the entire class.

**Room Setup**

Placement of each center was influenced by function and need (Figure 2.1). I considered a center's primary requirement, including access to water and/or electricity. I began charting these considerations. Messy 3D and Painting require convenient access to sinks in order to ensure efficient setup and cleanup. Sculpture requires access to four to six outlets to accommodate the use of hot glue guns, while Drawing & Coloring requires at least one outlet for the electric pencil sharpeners.

By viewing the classroom through the lens of student-studio space, I considered movement, transitions, and student independence. I visualized students gathering materials, accessing supplies, moving and storing projects, and cleaning up. I considered which materials and mediums may naturally be shared between centers and therefore should remain in close proximity to one another. I added these suppositions to my Studio Center Planning Guide and used this information to design a studio floor plan.

**Figure 2.1. West-facing view of classroom and studio arrangement**

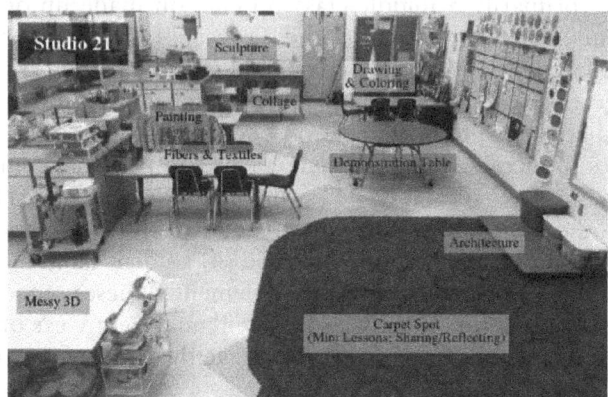

## Procedures and Expectations

Once I had completed the general classroom setup and studio design, I began to focus on classroom procedures and expectations. In a choice-based art room, routines maintain consistency, and the schedule is designed to offer students maximum time for independent studio exploration during their weekly art class. I divided each 45-minute class into four sections: (1) mini-lesson, (2) centers/student work time, (3) cleanup, and (4) sharing & reflection. I allotted 5 minutes each to cleanup and sharing/reflection, leaving 35 minutes for the mini-lesson and student work time. It became my goal to design and implement 5-minute mini-lessons, thus ensuring 30 minutes of student work time. I purchased a large visual timer and made color-coded anchor charts to represent our daily schedule. The expectations for each portion of time were included in each center, including noise levels and step-by-step procedures for each center. These clear visuals helped keep me accountable to my commitment to maximize student work time.

## Daily Schedule

After several weeks of implementing the schedule, cleanup and sharing/reflection were switched, inviting students to congregate at the carpet spot as soon as the timer went off, signaling the end of student work time. After sharing and reflection, students were directed as to where to store their artworks. Then they returned to the centers, which were eventually renamed Creation Stations, and completed cleanup. I had discovered that many students struggled to find a stopping point, regardless of being warned when work time was nearing an end. Because of this, students continued to work during cleanup, which then bled into sharing and reflection. I found that we were rarely left with more than 1 or 2 minutes of sharing time, but sharing and reflecting are vital components to the success of TAB and the growth of my artists.

Because students were excited to share their progress and creations, they came quickly to the carpet, according to the revised schedule. Once sharing and reflection had ended, students were no longer distracted by their creations and were able to focus on cleaning efficiently and cooperatively. Students were additionally motivated by the expectation that all Creation Stations must pass cleanup inspection by the time class was over. Any centers that did not meet expectations were closed during the following class period.

## Curriculum Design

I created a curriculum timeline of 10 weeks that integrated the selected themes (personal identity and community) and organized selected artists by theme (Table 2.1). I began by searching for and listing contemporary artists whose artworks were inspired by or expressed either personal identity or community. My intention was to select artists that represented diversity in style and medium, as well as gender, race, age, ethnicity, and cultural background. In addition to contemporary artists new to my students, including Lalla Essaydi and Duane Slick, I selected artists with whom I knew my students were familiar, such as Andy Warhol and Vincent Van Gogh. I paired artists thoughtfully, hoping to create interesting juxtapositions, thereby hastening the potential for thought-provoking comparisons.

**Table 2.1. Themes and Artists by Cycle Timeline**

| Cycle Day | Theme | Focus Artist(s) |
| --- | --- | --- |
| 1 | Introduction & Expectations | |
| 2 | Studio Exploration part 1 | |
| 3 | Studio Exploration part 2 | |
| 4 | Identity | Andy Warhol; Frida Kahlo; Glenn Ligon |
| 5 | Identity | Chuck Close; Lalla Essaydi |
| 6 | Identity | Kara Walker; Takashi Murakami |
| 7 | Identity | Amy Sherald; Duane Slick |
| 8 | Identity & Community | Ruby Onyinyechi Amanze; Matthew Cusick |
| 9 | Community | Vincent Van Gogh; Piet Mondrian; Gordon Matta-Clark |
| 10 | Community | Bettina Werner; Guillermo Kuitca |

## Student Handouts and Worksheets

My final preparation was to create the handouts and pre- and postsurveys that I used throughout the course of the study. Students completed a presurvey during Cycle Day 1 or 2. On Cycle Days 2 and 3 students explored Creation Stations, using the Creation Station Exploration Handout. During Creation Station exploration, students used this handout to document which centers they went to and what they did and/or created while there. Students were encouraged to include factual information as well as reflective journaling and sketching. During Cycle Day 4 students completed the Identity Worksheet (Figure 2.2). Depending on their progression, around Cycle Day 8 students were introduced to the WOW Planning Sheet. WOW stands for Wonderful Original Work and the concept originated from middle-school art teacher Barb Berry (Douglas & Jaquith, 2018). The WOW Planning Sheet was modeled after Berry's WOW expectations for engaging her students in high-quality creations.

By analyzing field notes, photos, student reflections, and work, authentic expression and self-exploration were themes of shared experience across grade levels. Students designed and created original pieces of artwork that were personally meaningful and revealing. Through their creations, students explored and expressed their interests, home lives, and aspirations. Postsurvey results revealed that 67% of students felt that they were able to

Figure 2.2. Identity Worksheet front and back. Students completed this section on the carpet and were given the option to choose which sections to complete.

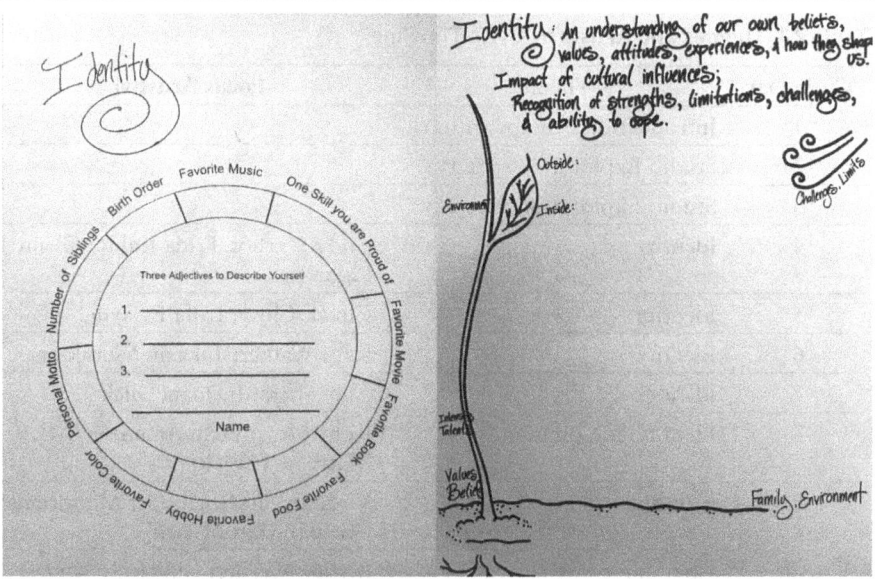

make choices and express themselves through the TAB setup most of the time or always. This was an increase from 44% of students who expressed these feelings during the presurvey.

As was expected with the transition from a teacher-directed curriculum to a student choice–based curriculum, students naturally collaborated, peer-taught, and demonstrated increased confidence and sagacity during sharing and reflection time. Students engaged in deeper conversations about their own artistic processes, as well as the motivations and creations of their fellow artists. Their actions and reflections demonstrated evidence of a sense of pride and personal accomplishment. Students continued to support each other as many worked through struggles with idea generation, craftsmanship, and adjusting to new routines and expectations. A true transformation was taking place within the walls of the studio, and the effects could be seen in student behavior, reflection, and artworks.

## AUTHENTIC EXPRESSION AND SELF-EXPLORATION

Students created original and personally meaningful artworks inspired by my selected themes. The first theme that was introduced was the theme of identity (refer to Table 2.1). In addition to learning about a variety of artists who represent identity throughout their own artworks, students engaged in conversations analyzing the different ways in which identity can be explored and synthesized. Students completed an "Identity Worksheet" (refer to Figure 2.2) as a way to begin documenting and exploring multiple facets of their personal identity. The worksheet helped guide students to consider exterior components, such as birth order and family ancestry, to more complex and personal categories, such as talents, fears, and personal challenges. I gave students the option to fold their completed worksheet as an indication that they did not want it to be read by teachers or peers. This recourse promoted the opportunity for students to explore and record information that was personal or sensitive without leaving them feeling vulnerable or overexposed. The majority of students left their sheets unfolded and were eager to share and compare aspects of their perceived identities with their classmates and me.

Students demonstrated authentic expression and self-exploration by representing aspects of real-life circumstances and describing personal feelings and thoughts aligned with their visuals.

A 5th-grader named Austin chose to focus on the theme of personal identity. He initially struggled to generate a project idea and to complete his WOW planning sheet. Austin came to me frustrated after spending the majority of the class feeling immobilized. I encouraged him to consider the station and supplies he was most interested in working with, since he was struggling to generate an original idea. A classmate indicated that he was looking for a partner who would help him construct a papier-mâché mask

**Figure 2.3. Austin's mask, work in progress**

(Figure 2.3). Austin eagerly agreed to be his partner and exhibited signs of relief that he had a starting point. Since creating the mask base would take two full art periods, Austin had additional time to consider how he might express personal identity through the design. Once the masks were ready to design, he struggled once again, expressing that he didn't know what to do with it. I suggested he refer back to his Identity Sheet.

Austin explained the connection between his identity and project idea by sharing:

> I didn't really know what I should do but then Louis needed a partner so I decided to make a mask. But then I didn't know what to turn it into so Miss Sandra told me go read my sheet where I wrote about myself and stuff and it gave me the idea of being invisible like a ghost so I started to make a ghost . . . but then I got this idea about secrets and I thought I could turn my mouth into a door and put keys on each side . . . and Miss Sandra said she could get me some. And so if you use one key I will tell the truth and if you use the other key I will tell you a lie. I'm not done but I'm gonna make the door so it really opens and if someone picks the truth-key it doesn't even matter cause I'm a ghost . . . I'm invisible. (personal communication, October 2018)

Austin began expressing and symbolizing abstract thoughts and emotions, as indicated by his verbal explanation. When describing his mask, he

**Figure 2.4. Callie's community-inspired collage**

spoke in the first person, indicative of an intimate connection between his artwork and his personal identity.

Callie, a 1st-grader, focused on community and created a collage of her house and the street she lived on (Figure 2.4). She talked openly about aspects of her hometown, her family, and which windows coincided with each family member's bedroom. During reflection time, Callie described her composition to a peer saying, "This is my mom's house. This is dad's house. My mom and dad live apart. My dad lives far, far away but I just wanted to put him right here, in one picture" (personal communication, October 25, 2018).

Wren, a 5th-grader, created a mixed media sculpture of a beloved structure in her hometown that had been recently torn down (Figure 2.5).

**Figure 2.5. Wren's community-inspired mixed-media sculpture**

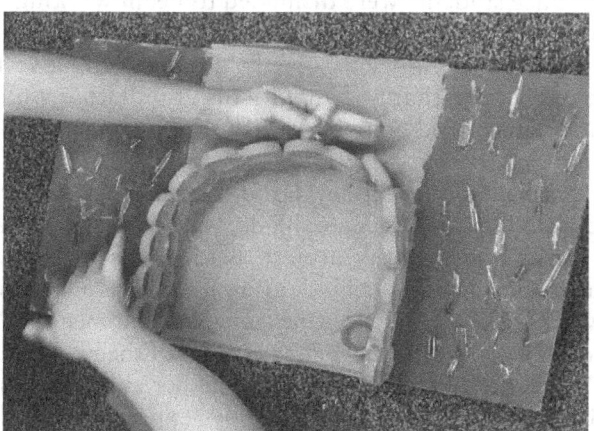

The memories of the community landmark were important to her even though the structure was no longer physically a part of her community. She expressed this by telling a classmate:

> Even though the mousehole isn't there anymore it's still a part of the town. Like we're still having Melvin Mousehole Days. It's where all the Melvin kids meet to go sledding and ride bikes down. And you know Mrs. Dailey who used to work here? Yeah, she was my mom's teacher and her kids slid down it too. It's weird that it's not there but it was going to cost too much to fix . . . so this is fun to build. (personal communication, November 6, 2018)

The use of meaningful themes, such as identity and community, provided students with a platform to generate and express personally consequential matters.

## CONNECTIONS THROUGH SHARED EXPERIENCES

During sharing and reflection, students made comparisons between their personal artworks and the artworks of peers and of the artists introduced during mini-lessons. As students found similarities, they began to discuss the commonalities regarding their experiences, feelings, and ideas that they shared with others. Through these comparisons, students learned to connect with others on a deeper, more meaningful level. These connections promote empathy, communication, and critical thinking. Transitioning to a choice-based curriculum naturally encouraged an atmosphere of peer collaboration. Incorporating themes revealed congruities among peers that had previously remained undiscovered. During the initial personal-identity warm-up, students created mini artworks expressing their identities. Jarod, a 5th-grade student, was ecstatic, verbalizing that he already had several ideas. Once students were dismissed to begin working, Jarod asked to borrow my computer to look up the Union Pacific logo. As he selected an image and began working, he openly discussed his love for the railroad and the connection that he had with his grandfather who also shared his interest in trains. Jarod completed his artwork with intense focus and captivation.

During sharing and reflection, Jarod's excitement was compounded when he discovered that a classmate, Blade, was also expressing his love for the railroad through his identity project. Blade shared, "I've always loved trains and the track runs right behind our house." Classmates were eager to use their artworks as comparisons. One classmate commented, "That's cool, they both picked to do train stuff but then both of their pictures turned out so different." Another classmate inquired whether either boy knew that the other was also interested in trains. Both boys expressed that the discovery

**Figure 2.6. Classmates Blade and Jarod collaborate on a WOW sculpture**

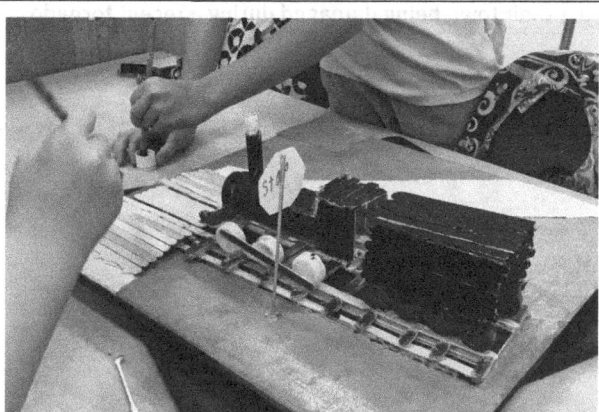

was a new one, Jarod adding, "And we've even gone to school together since kindergarten."

When the WOW planning sheet was introduced, Jarod and Blade approached me immediately to ask if they could work together on one project. After a brief discussion of expectations, the boys enthusiastically planned a community-themed collaborative sculpture (Figure 2.6). Discovering a shared interest that each student related to his personal identity became a bridge to collaboratively explore the theme of community within their artwork.

Just as Blade and Jarod's sculpture suggests, meaningful themes promote a culture of human connection through shared experiences. This effect was similarly revealed during a community-themed art challenge. I divided students into groups based on their hometown. Using blocks from the architecture Creation Station, I instructed students to work collaboratively with their group to create a sculpture to represent their community. During the art challenge, students were engaged and exhibited impressive communication and cooperation skills.

A particular group lived in a town that had recently been hit by a tornado. Students worked together to create a representation of the main street through town, where much of the damage had occurred, including the courthouse tower, which had been knocked down (Figure 2.7). Students in this group took turns reenacting their interpretation of the day that the storm struck. Swirling their fingers and dragging them across the town, the children described where the tornado traveled and which buildings had been struck and destroyed. Each would then knock over the blocks as they narrated the storyline. Members recounted to each other where they were, what they were thinking, and how they were feeling. They opened up to each

**Figure 2.7. Fourth-graders turn a collaborative sculpture into performance art as they reenact their town being damaged during a recent tornado**

other about their fears, hopes, and experience. Then they rebuilt the structure together and the next group member took his or her turn. One student followed the community art challenge by creating artworks focused on positive slogans about strength, rebuilding, and community.

Connecting through shared experiences was reinforced during class discussions, which occurred during the opening mini-lesson portion of the class and during sharing and reflection at the end. During these discussions, I encouraged students to compare and contrast the artworks of professional artists, as well as the artworks created in class by peers and themselves. I guided students to discuss the differences among artworks that shared similarities in themes. I also encouraged students to examine commonalities among artworks that initially appeared to be very different. Through these discussions, students opened up and bonded over shared experiences. Lillia, a 2nd-grade artist, summed it up simply and eloquently by saying:

> We all are the same and we all are different. No matter what it looks like we can use our eyes and our brains to find what's the same and to find what's different. And being different is being special but we are still connected. (personal communication, October 2018)

After being dismissed to free choice Creation Stations, Lillia began to create a drawing (Figure 2.8). When asked about her drawing, she responded, "What are those one things called again? You know . . . the two circles for sames and differences?" Lillia was reminded that she was referring to a Venn diagram. "Yeah! One of those! I am making a Venn diagram about two artists I know . . . and I'm one of them."

**Figure 2.8. Lillia's Venn diagram drawing**

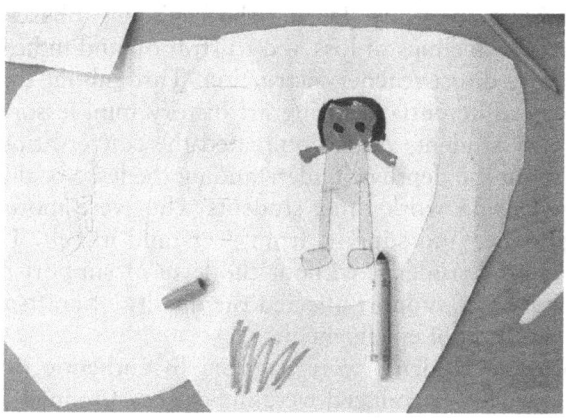

Finally, the direction themes guided the students, while still preserving choice and authentic meaning. Postsurvey results indicate that 82% of students described their ideal way of creating during art class as including at least an even mixture of student choice and teacher-directed lessons.

## CONCLUSIONS

Incorporating meaningful themes for art making into a choice-based elementary art curriculum provides a platform for authentic expression and self-exploration, and promotes a culture of connection through shared experiences. As I described in this chapter, 1st- through 5th-grade students in my art classroom experienced the beginning stages of the transition from a teacher-directed setup into a choice-based approach. Themes of personal identity and community were introduced and incorporated into the new curriculum and setup. Themes were reinforced by the introduction and discussion of specially selected artists and artworks. Art history incorporation and warmup art challenges acted as springboards for class discussion and long-term WOW projects.

This study reinforces current research that indicates the potential for implementing TAB and student choice. Students developed and increased their skills relating to communication, problem-solving, creativity, and autonomy (Douglas & Jaquith, 2018; Jaquith, 2012). Few studies offer insights to ensure a successful transition from a teacher-directed elementary art curriculum to TAB. A choice-based curriculum provides a foundation to utilize meaningful themes. In return, meaningful themes guided the transition to a TAB model curriculum by providing a springboard for holistic idea generation and art history connections.

I learned alongside my students and made continual adjustments and changes throughout my study. During the beginning phases, several students struggled with feelings of loss and frustration and indicated that they would prefer more direct teacher instruction. Throughout the study I also noted the need to differentiate during art history mini-lessons and discussions. High-ability students often dominated the conversations, and I was left uncertain about the depth of understanding the less vocal students were demonstrating. During work time, students who were more assertive received more guidance and support from peers and myself. This left many of the more reserved students without the level of support needed in the beginning. This lack of support affected the quality of craftsmanship, time management, and level of engagement.

The majority of students were engaged in authentic expression and creativity. The artworks produced were indicative of individual student interest, choice, and skill level. Increased student autonomy also resulted in collaboration and peer teaching. As time went on, students and I became more familiar with the new setup and expectations. The quality and creativity of the students' artwork increased along with their confidence, especially for those who initially struggled. Using meaningful themes provided a framework for the new curriculum and laid a foundation for conversations comparing a diverse range of artists and artworks.

Art teachers who are interested in shifting to a choice-based approach may benefit from incorporating meaningful themes into their curriculum. Educators interested in facilitating opportunities for students to engage in authentic expression and/or increase the culture of human connections through shared experiences may also benefit from this study.

Designing the core of an elementary choice-based art curriculum around identity and community provides a more significant platform for students in their decision-making process. While skills and theory continue to be embedded into daily practice, they no longer become the driving force of the projects being created. Through the use of meaningful themes and a choice-based approach, teachers may find a viable option for offering their brilliant artists a more worthy "why" in an environment designed to keep them safe and let them fly.

## REFERENCES

Anderson, T., & Milbrandt, M. (1998). Authentic instruction in art: Why and how to dump the school art style. *Visual Arts Research*, 24(1), 13–20. https://www.jstor.org/stable/20715931

Arao, B., & Clemens, K. (2013). From safe spaces to brave spaces. In L. M. Landreman (Ed.), *The art of effective facilitation* (pp. 135–150). Stylus Publishing, LLC.

Creswell, J. W. (2013). *Research design: Qualitative, quantitative, and mixed methods approaches* (4th ed.). SAGE Publications, Inc.

Douglas, K. M. (2012). Advocating for a student-centered art program. In D. B. Jaquith & N. E. Hathaway (Eds.), *The learner-directed classroom: Developing creative thinking skills through art* (pp. 9–17). Teachers College Press.

Douglas, K. M., & Jaquith, D. B. (2018). *Engaging learners through artmaking: Choice-based art education in the classroom (TAB)*. Teachers College Press.

Efland, A. (1976). The school art style: A functional analysis. *Studies in Art Education, 17*(2), 37–44. https://doi.org/10.2307/1319979

Gude, O. (2013). New school art styles: The project of art education. *Art Education, 66*(1), 6–15. https://doi.org/10.1080/00043125.2013.11519203

Hathaway, N. E., & Jaquith, D. B. (2014). Where's the revolution? *Phi Delta Kappan, 95*(N6), 25–29.

Jaquith, D. B. (2012). Time as a choice in self-directed learning. In D. B. Jaquith & N. E. Hathaway (Eds.), *The learner-directed classroom: Developing creative thinking skills through art* (pp. 18–29). Teachers College Press.

Jaquith, D. B., & Hathaway, N. E. (2012). *The learner-directed classroom: Developing creative thinking skills through art*. Teachers College Press.

Mertens, D. M. (2003). Mixed methods and the politics of human research: The transformative-emancipatory perspective. In A. Tashakkori & C. Teddlie (Eds.), *Handbook of mixed methods in social and behavioral research* (pp. 135–164). Sage.

Pellish, J. (2012). Past, present, future: Stories of identity in an elementary art room. *Art Education, 65*(1), 19–24. https://doi.org/10.1080/00043125.2012.11519156

Sweetman, D., Badiee, M., & Creswell, J. W. (2010). Use of the transformative framework in mixed methods studies. *Qualitative Inquiry, 16*(6), 441–454.

Walker, S. (2004). Understanding the artmaking process: Reflective practice. *Art Education, 57*(3), 6–12. https://doi.org/10.1080/00043125.2004.11653545

CHAPTER 3

# Learning Choices
## Students in a Flipped Art Room

*Kathryn Christensen*

Art educators are masters of navigating a busy and active environment. We hold the attention of an entire class with one demonstration. We smile at the sight of hands in paint and clay. We use failures and struggles as tools for our students to become self-reliant and resilient learners. While organizing chaos is what art educators do (see Figure 3.1 and Figure 3.2 for this teacher's dream), there are always ways to improve teaching practice. It is possible to reach students with different skill levels at one time. Students are able to become independent learners and trust their own learning path. Teachers can meet 21st-Century Learning Standards (Iowa Core, n.d.a) and save planning time by developing a scaffolded teaching curriculum for a virtual classroom.

"Flipping the classroom" refers to a student-centered teaching method in which teachers prepare an online scaffolded curriculum for students to complete outside of class. This method opens with in-class time for collaborative and one-to-one learning. This method can relieve many teaching challenges. Demonstrations and presentations online mitigate for student absences, and allow for more individualized instruction. Since teachers are tasked with providing an environment in which students must develop independent learning skills under the Iowa Core 21st-Century Learning Standards, developing independent learning habits where students are asked to view recordings in advance cultivate habits such as time management, and help develop self-advocacy, responsibility, and work ethic.

In my own practice, using a modified flipped classroom method has been important for addressing demonstrations, brainstorming, discussion, guided instruction, feedback, collaboration, reflection, and differentiation. This approach allowed me to utilize parts of traditional flipped teaching methods (online scaffolding), adapt those to classroom needs, and provide individualized pacing for students. It allowed students the freedom to work at their own pace. During the time of my research, I observed how this modified flipped approach was impacted by changes caused by COVID-19. As always, there were learning successes and struggles. The

**Figure 3.1. *The Teacher's Dream, 2020: Part 1.* Drawing by the author.**

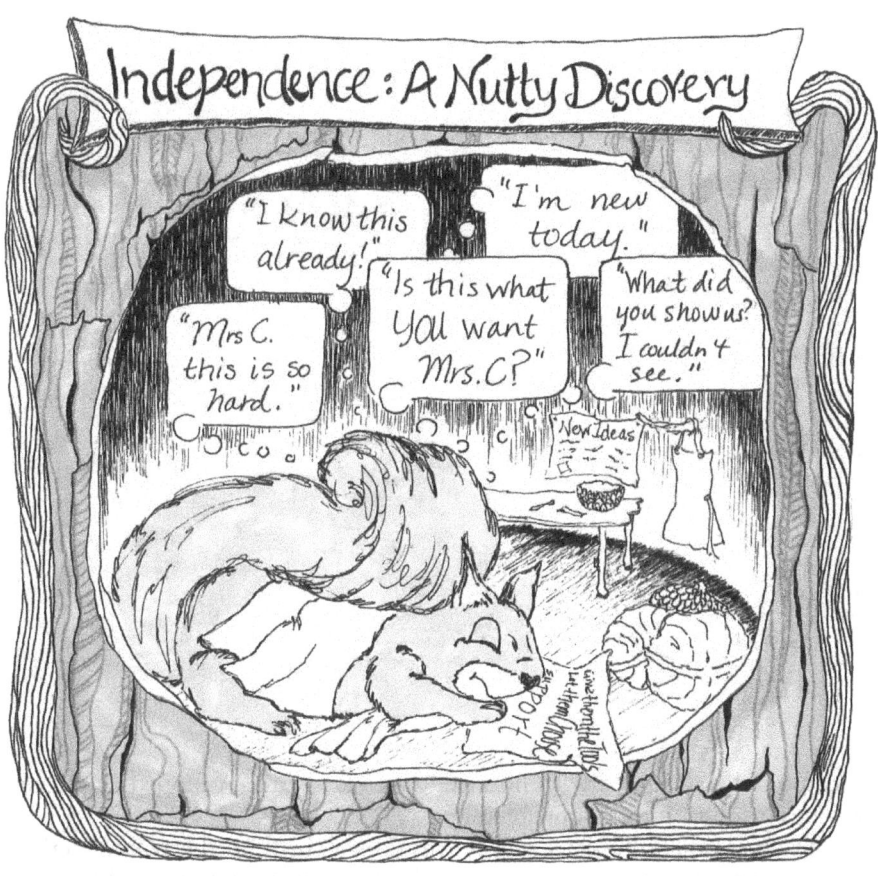

flipped experience aims to involve student motivation and enable students to gain independence, learn to take risks, meet personal expectations, and set goals at their own pace, as well as include countless time-saving practices.

    I want students to grow in ability (no matter their skill level), realize their time matters, have confidence, become independent, and take ownership in their learning. As students move into middle school, they need to learn to make choices, problem solve, and understand the effects of their actions so they are prepared for high school and life beyond K–12 education. Many students seem unsure in their choices and have a lack of initiative to investigate, problem solve, and take risks. At the same time, there is a portion of students that are prepared and ready to learn. In a non-flipped classroom, much of my class time was spent with students who were absent or behind in their work. The prepared students were left to themselves, and

**Figure 3.2. *The Teacher's Dream, 2020: Part 2.*** **Drawing by the author.**

unfortunately, struggled with unproductive class time. A flipped classroom provides a solution to this problem.

In two middle-school art classrooms, I used the flipped learning method as a way for students to investigate and reflect on their individual learning path. I studied student choices and learning discovery as well as identified the strategies that help students achieve independence and self-identify as successful through their learning process. I investigated strategy choices by asking:

- What are the outcomes when middle school students select their own learning path and individualize their learning?
- In what ways can students individualize their own learning?

I investigated independence and self-identification/reflection by asking:

- Can flipped learning help students individualize and contemplate their own art making?
- Does flipped learning motivate students to make independent choices?

## BENEFITS OF THE FLIPPED CLASSROOM

The flipped classroom method provides advantages to art teachers, their students, and parents in many ways including efficient planning, developing scaffolded instruction, and creating an active learning environment that supports 21st-century learning.

First, the flipped method provides an efficient way to plan. One study found that although "teachers spent 2 hours per topic to create videotaped lectures and digital slide presentations with voice overs, [they] found preparation time was significantly reduced after the initial groundwork was completed" (Roehl et al., 2013, p. 46). While the initial planning is intensive and intimidating, customizing curriculum is second nature to art teachers (Delacruz, 2009). As tutorials are created, organized, and edited, prep time is saved for student feedback and differentiation.

Scaffolding and differentiating instruction for all students in the art room can be challenging. Today's art room composition ranges from English language learners (ELLs) and students struggling with fine motor skills to students who could instruct the art teacher. All these students deserve to be growing and learning every moment when they cross into the art room. Differentiated learning through flipping the art classroom provides custom instruction for all students. During traditional classroom instruction, teachers often deliver information too quickly for some and too slowly for others (Morgan, 2014). Through the use of online video tutorials, directions, and guided work time, instruction can be delivered at the students' own pace and skill level, as well as providing student control over individual pacing. This advantage allows the art teacher to reach struggling students, ELLs, and multiple skill levels within the class time. It also helps students learn how they learn, and be more self efficacious. In one art classroom, for instance, a student was not able to break free from mimicry. The flipped method allowed the teacher to differentiate learning for the individual student through guidance and immediate feedback while others worked independently (Hopper, 2016).

Our ultimate goal as educators should be to help students become self-sufficient and independent learners. As educators, we know student-centered pedagogy encourages student engagement and motivation. Students enjoy and grow through choice-based, student-centered assignments. If executed correctly, the flipped method offers art students multi-layered personalized instruction to guide their own artistic learning.

## COMPONENTS OF A FLIPPED CLASSROOM

Each flipped classroom will look different based on the teacher and their students. The success of a flipped classroom is dependent on four factors: the teacher, the student, the device in use, and the family. Without cooperation, the method may break down.

## The Teacher

First, teachers must be willing to shift their attitude and adapt traditional instruction (Roehl et al., 2013; Varier et al., 2017). The 1:1 initiatives and learning management systems adopted by school districts have created a viable opportunity for educators to begin the flipped classroom journey. Teachers must also remember that this method is not foolproof, and general best practices in pedagogy must be used in combination with the flipped method. A teacher cannot expect a student to know when and how to use videos without modeling first. Explicit instruction is crucial in flipping the classroom; tutorials cannot replace quality teaching, and students need to learn how to navigate and interact with the tutorials. Students can work independently if modeling and providing high expectations are guided by the teacher (Hopper, 2016). Roehling et al. (2017) emphasized that teachers must approach flipping with caution to ensure it is used appropriately and benefits all students.

Within the flipped method, a range of online tools and strategies can be utilized to fit teacher and student styles. No classroom is identical. Lage et al. (2000) researched and compiled literature on learning styles, personality styles, and processing styles. Learning styles refers to whether a student is dependent, collaborative, or independent within the classroom. The four personality styles are: Introvert or Extrovert; Sensing or Intuitive; Thinking or Feeling; and Judging or Perceiving. How a student processes information is divided into four categories: assimilators, convergers, divergers, and accommodators. This research explains why classroom teachers cannot reach all student learning needs at the same time, why some students fall through the cracks, and why flipped learning "can appeal to all types of learners" (p. 32). Each student group creates a new dynamic, and the teacher must adapt. This versatile range of tools for flipping the classroom includes the following but is not limited to videotaped lectures, screen-capture with voiceover, digital presentations, YouTube videos, discipline-specific websites, research-based instructional videos (like Khan Academy), and game-based instructional websites. The tools generalized by Roehl et al. (2013) can improve communication and connection with students and have the ability to meet the varying styles, as cited by Lage et al. (2000). As tools change and evolve, professional development is needed to adjust to meet new learning curves.

## The Student

As a teacher begins to develop flipped classroom resources, there are several student issues that can present a challenge. For the flipped classroom to function, students must use a device with Internet accessibility. Herein lies the basis of the main limitation of implementing a flipped classroom related to students. Limitations found through research are:

- Students' unwillingness to do the work (Roehling et al., 2017)
- Lack of Internet access at home (Bergmann & Sams, 2012; Roehl et al., 2013; Varier et al., 2017)
- Broken devices before, during, and/or at the end of class (Varier et al., 2017)
- More distraction at home (Roehling et al., 2017)
- Students' inability to self-regulate their learning (Cheng et al., 2018)

Each of these struggles, while justified challenges, are not new. No matter the tool (Chromebook, clay tool, or pencil), some students always find a way to avoid productivity, and it can be the teacher, their methods, and classroom management that helps to guide student learning.

**The Device and the Internet**

The third piece in this puzzle is the device itself. No matter how well a teacher has planned, how wonderful the tutorial, how well behaved students are, the device and its functionality are crucial. Tech support works very quickly to fix requests as fast as they can. Educators cannot control incompatibility snafus (Delacruz, 2009). We can, however, adapt just as every other teacher has before us. Teaching will always require flexibility and innovative thinking. Art teachers must be primed and ready to roll when plans go awry.

**Parents and Family**

The flipped classroom method reaches more than students (Fulton, 2012; Morgan, 2014); it supports the family. There can be a separation between school and home, but when the two are blended and collaboration begins, student growth and understanding between parents and teachers form. Parental support is a crucial part of success in the classroom. Fulton (2012) stated that a Minnesota district in 2009 found that 84 percent of parents preferred the flipped classroom as the instructional method. It gave the parents insight into their child's learning. It also helped them understand the approach and/or the strategy their child's teacher used in the classroom. While this research was based on a math curriculum, implementing a transparent curriculum and instructional strategy would be beneficial to all content areas including the arts. Bergmann and Sams's (2012) book shares an extraordinary flipped classroom testimony from a kindergarten teacher at a conference. The teacher sent iPods home with ELL students and the devices came back drained. Later at parent-teacher conferences, the teacher discovered that the whole family was learning to read through this new flipped strategy. The flipped classroom provides support and stability for students, especially during a time such as COVID-19. Collaboration between parents and teachers is the most essential tool for the students to grow. Through these methods we can see how successful a flipped classroom can be for not just our students, but our parents as well.

## MAKING IT WORK: A FLIPPED ART ROOM CASE STUDY

The art room is an active environment—one with loud thoughts, struggles, and successes.

In the 2020 school year, COVID-19 presented many challenges, but I continued my plan to document student experiences within my flipped art classroom. In the district where I teach, the demographics have shifted in the last 20 years from a predominantly White population to a minority enrollment of 69% (majority Hispanic), which is more than the Iowa public school average of 24% (Iowa Department of Education, 2020). In our district ELLs are at 40.20%, and at the middle school level, 32%. The migrant population is at 6.7% for the district, and our free or reduced lunch population is 71%.

Because of the pandemic, parents were given the option of enrolling their child(ren) in on-site learning or online learning. At the middle school level 68 students were enrolled in online learning and 547 enrolled in on-site learning. Each day the numbers shifted as parents elected to pull their child from the in-person classroom (on-site learning) and complete learning at home, or move from virtual to on-site learning.

Nonetheless, I decided to study student outcomes when middle school art students select their own learning path and individualize their learning, and in what ways students can individualize their own learning. Still, challenges included not only the technological, but also the vagaries of changing policies and student absences. It should also be noted that the social and emotional state of students may have affected their experience. I kept individual art processes, work time, and self-reflections (in and out of the art classroom) as stable as possible, but each student was dealing with worries due to the pandemic. Despite these limitations, students (and I) took changes in stride. In fact, we all adapted just as Bandura's (1989) theory suggests.

Through a modified flipped method (blend of the flipped method and direct instruction methods), I gave 37 8th-grade students a set of requirements for each project and a due date. Within that time frame, I taught students using in-person demonstrations as well as prerecorded videos, guided practice, and independent work time. Each student managed

Learning Choices

their learning choices; they decided when they needed more dependent instruction and when they felt they could work independently (at their own pace). Students were aware of their learning choices through a learning checklist tracker (Figure 3.3). The checklist categorized three learning styles: dependent, collaborative, independent. As students created and reflected on their art, they filled out the checklist. The checklist gave students the freedom to choose their path, track their choices, find a way to reflect and analyze those actions, and finally repeat so they could grow from their

**Figure 3.3. Learning Checklist, 2021**

# Learning Checklist

Name (first and last) _____

Date _____ Class Period _____

You will be learning about your own learning style this year as you create in this class. Which learning choices help you learn best? Is Mrs. C providing the help you need to succeed? Does one learning style choice work in combination wth another? Each student is different.

Directions:
-As Mrs. C asks, you will fill out the checklist below to track your learning choices. Check all choices you make throughout the class. There are no wrong or right choices. Just be honest with yourself.

| Dependent | Collaborative | Independent |
|---|---|---|
| ____Used Mrs. C's idea. | ____Chatted with a classmate about different ideas. | ____Asked a question because I had a new idea. |
| ____Needed help to start. Not sure how to begin. Asked Mrs. C what to do next. | ____Asked a friend what the next step was. | ____Looked on Canvas/Art Website before asking a question. |
| ____I worked alone or with someone but didn't get very far. | ____Worked with a partner and got a lot done. | ____I worked alone. I got a lot done. |
| ____Someone in class helped me. | ____I worked with someone in class. We helped each other. | ____I worked alone on this part. If someone needed help, I helped them. |
| ____I prefer to have Mrs. C's help or one classmate. I follow what they do or say. | ____I prefer to work with a classmate and learn things together. | ____I prefer to work things out on my own. I check the website first for understanding. |
| ____I didn't share any ideas. | ____I shared an idea with a classmate. | ____I kept my idea to myself. |
| ____I didn't do any work outside of class. | ____I talked about my project idea with a classmate out of class. | ____I watched a video or read directions outside of class. |
| ____I was missing materials. | ____I shared materials. | ____I found my own tutorial video to help me. |
| ____ | ____ | ____I answered Mrs. C's questions as I walked in the room and I began working right as I got to class. |
| ____ | ____ | ____I was prepared with my materials. |
| ____ | ____ | ____I sent an email outside of class about this project. |
| ____ | ____ | ____ |
| ____ | ____ | ____ |

Reflection: Answer the following questions.
1. From which learning style did I select the most choices? _____
2. What is one learning change I will make in the next project? _____
3. What learning choice was the most effective? _____

**Figure 3.4. Ranked Learning Choices, 2021**

| | | Ranked Learning Choices |
|---|---|---|
| **Independent** | 20 | Helped another student. |
| | 19 | Found own tutorial for own idea. Took a risk. |
| | 18 | Watched a video/tutorial on own time. Worked at home. |
| | 17 | Prefers to work alone. Got a lot done. Made edits on own. |
| | 16 | Checked canvas/website for understanding first. |
| | 15 | Prepared for class. |
| **Collaborative** | 14 | Chatted w/ teacher about a different direction. |
| | 13 | Sent an email out of class for clarification. |
| | 12 | Asked for clarification in class. |
| | 11 | Asked teacher about a new idea. |
| | 10 | Talked w/ a classmate outside of class about the project. |
| | 9 | Prefers to work w/ a classmate or learn together. |
| | 8 | Worked w/ a classmate. Got a lot done. |
| | 7 | Chatted with a classmate about the project. |
| | 6 | Asked a friend for help. |
| | 5 | Prefers teacher's help/clarification. |
| **Dependent** | 4 | Copied teacher's idea. |
| | 3 | Needed the teacher to begin. Prompted by the teacher. |
| | 2 | Didn't ask for help when needed. Not productive. Wasted time. |
| | 1 | Not prepared. Didn't check email at the start of class. Forget materials. |

experiences. Through the use of the learning checklist tracker, students were more aware of the choices they could personally make each day. Students used Ranked Learning Choices (Figure 3.4) to determine if their learning style had changed over time. This is not a comprehensive list; it was meant to be a manageable list of choices for the students within the time frame of the art class. Students were given the checklist tracker at the beginning of each project. They selected their learning choices (could be 1 or more) at the beginning, middle, and end of each project, using different colors to distinguish choices that may have changes during the project. Finally, students reflected on what learning styles they used throughout the project by examining the Ranked Learning Choices sheet and answering prompts such as "What is your strength? What could you improve upon?"

From the checklist and ranked data, a variety of student learning paths emerged that support success through student choice. Motivation and engagement, student communication, and teacher support were all necessary for student growth. Student surveys, interviews, and reflections showed these teacher-driven factors integrated with student-driven factors that included choice, environment, and ownership. I selected a narrower set of findings to elucidate how a subset of eight particular students created their own learning paths. Each student discussed below struggled within the school setting due to academic, behavioral, or emotional reasons. Five students were identified (Students 2, 3, 4, 6, and 8) with repetitive behavior issues (unproductive, unprepared, distracts others, lack of personal space, disengaged) that occur in more than just the art class. Student 7 is a special education student with an Individualized Education Plan (IEP) in reading and math and required extra processing time. The remaining 2 students (Students 1 and 5) struggle with social emotional issues and self-confidence; they have developed a sense of learned helplessness. Based on their work and my observations, all these students demonstrated growth in individual learning choices as well as independent skills and habits. What I found is that independent learning is comprised of teacher support and scaffolding, student ownership, and resilience.

## TEACHER SUPPORT AND SCAFFOLDING

The flipped method is only as effective as the teacher in the classroom. What does each student need from the teacher to develop ownership, resilience, and self-efficacy? How does a student view support? My students made it very clear that the teacher should support, encourage, and guide. Throughout the 8 weeks, many students stated, "I can work because it is quiet in here" or "Thanks for the email you sent. It helps me get prepared before class" or "Mrs. C taught me that it's okay to make mistakes and that sometimes mistakes can make your project/situation better." Statements such as these are confirmation that as much as the student may want a teacher to rescue them, resilience and self-efficacy is developed through practice. A teacher cannot steal a student's struggle. This does not mean students are left to fend for themselves, but rather they try first with the knowledge the teacher will be there for support.

I found that students need a teacher to help them be resilient, show self-efficacy, and become independent. First, they need the teacher to prepare and deliver instruction multiple ways for all students. Second, the classroom environment must be positive, safe, and consistent. Third, the teacher must develop a positive and collaborative relationship with the students. While each of these requirements seems like common sense, the flipped classroom method has allowed me to meet their needs and help achieve my goals for them.

### Planning and Instructional Delivery

The teacher must prepare online tutorials, directions, and links before a student is ready to start the project. While time is a burden at first, the teacher will soon feel accomplishment and success due to the prepared nature of this method. During class, the teacher must be able to balance the scaffolding at any moment. There will be a shifting need for one-on-one instruction and independent learning. One student stated, "She goes around the room to help students when they are struggling." This will allow students to move ahead while others are not ready. Meaning, there will be a bit of chaos at times, but it is organized chaos. This year, I decided to try sending an email before class to students weekly (sometimes multiple times a week) to help cut down on digital clicking and confusion. Our district uses Canvas as a learning management system that requires lots of navigation and understanding. When I asked students how often they read emails to be prepared outside of class, 50% utilized the email every time it was available and 34% used it at least once a week. This means that almost 85% of my students want to be prepared before class so that we can start immediately. Two students honestly stated, "I would rather know what to do beforehand and come to class more prepared" and "I feel like I learn quicker rather than having to wait." If students have planned and brainstormed and the teacher has built in online scaffolding, every student will be engaged, feel more supported, and therefore develop a sense of responsibility because they have been given a chance to take ownership of their learning. As stated before, students will also feel more inclined to take a chance if they are supported through scaffolding.

As a teacher builds the online scaffolding, it is important to develop tutorials for multiple skill levels, not just process tutorials to create a finished project. When asked how my tutorials motivate students during class, one student said, "They help me figure out how to do challenging things." As we live in a digital world, teachers all know that tutorials can either assist and guide or just waste the student's time. This student appreciated the ability to challenge themselves through a selection of tutorials that I made available to all students. A challenge doesn't always mean that an advanced student is going above and beyond. In fact, it is important to remember that each of our students can be challenged at all levels through the flipped method, which in turn will help each student create self-efficacy and resilience.

**Creating the Classroom Environment**

Every student, when interviewed, shared that the art environment was very important for motivation and independence; a space that creates a routine so students know what to expect. The student can just *be* in the space without having to learn to maneuver through classroom management issues. The flipped method also removes many classroom management issues. Many students suggested they struggle in other classes because they are bored or the class is moving too quickly. As I have established, this method provides learning at the student's pace and at their skill level. Problematic behaviors are virtually nonexistent. If I see a behavior issue in class, it really isn't an issue for long. Most of my students ignore it because they are too invested in their own work to give the behavior the importance that the culprit expects.

## Positive Relationship and Communication

Building a positive relationship with each student is vital. The student must be able to trust that they will be supported. Just as the themes I discovered from student observations, interviews, and their learning path are intertwined, the planning, instructional delivery, and environment help build a positive relationship with students. The flipped method provides time for individual guidance, help, and redirection as all other students are engaged and working independently. This cultivates genuine relationships through trust and honesty because each student's need is met through feedback, a conversation or discussion, and personal editing critiques. One student stated, "Mrs. C gives me great advice and reminds me to keep going." In this way, the student-centered nature of flipping the classroom also makes students feel safe asking questions of their teacher and classmates because it becomes a one-to-one environment.

## STUDENT OWNERSHIP

## Self-Advocacy

Students advocated for themselves through the flipped classroom process and in turn developed self-efficacy. Self-efficacy is "another cognitive factor that plays an influential role in the exercise of personal control over motivation." (Bandura, 1989, p. 47). In a sense, this teaching method allowed students to create their own voices by self-navigating and becoming their own guides as independent, individual learners. Because of the open and self-guided approach and the creative nature of the art classroom, students had to become their own advocates. For example, the learning path for Student 7 suggests that advocating for oneself has a big impact on independence as well as developing ownership of learning. As students practice self-advocacy skills, they will naturally begin to question, revise, edit, and self-reflect without prompting.

When asked how his learning style changed over the 8 weeks, Student 7 shared, "My learning style changed because I was comfortable when I asked for help. I was able to know what I was doing." This was a breakthrough for this student. During previous years, he would wait for me to come to him to help edit or analyze and then move on. Another student stated, "I started to ask more questions before my learning style changed." In this way, the flexibility of the flipped method provides students the time to become comfortable in the space. This method clearly helped both students create a new comfort level when speaking up.

**Collaboration**

Students sought clarification, collaborated with peers and the teacher about ideas, questioned themselves and each other, and chatted with classmates throughout the creative process. Chatting may seem like unproductive learning at first glance; however, in many cases this is the student's most comfortable way to reflect, edit, and revise in a safe and consistent learning environment. Student 4 is an example of how a collaborative student learns within a flipped learning method of teaching. This type of student is dependent on others for motivation and investment in the learning process. Many students openly stated that they worked best when they could "bounce ideas off" one another.

Collaboration can also hinder independent thinking and learning. One student did not select to do much out-of-school process work. It is possible that restrictions due to COVID-19 had more of an impact in the at-home setting. In any case, this type of learning creates a comfortable learning environment and allows the students to become a sounding board for others. While the flipped classroom allows this type of learning, both students and teachers need to be aware that when the collaborative environment shifts to dependency, learning is not productive or engaging. I found it effective to scaffold skills and habits that enabled collaborative learners to practice independent thinking.

Asking students to write a goal is an effective and simple way to keep students focused on their own effort and investment; the teacher should check in with each student. Student 5 stated, "Mrs. C helps us by answering our questions quickly and letting us work." Students were most responsive to make the conversation light and informal. In comparing the learning paths of Student 2 and Student 5, Student 2 had a more collaborative learning style.

When this student decided to take a break from collaboration (Week 6), his independent skills kicked in. He stated, "I want to be more focused on my work." This student made responsible communication choices in his learning path that guided him successfully through to the end of the class. In contrast, Student 5 was more independent in nature even at the beginning of the class. She utilized more teacher communication and was able to make use of self-reflective skills earlier on in the class. During Week 8, my findings reveal that this student became completely independent at the end of the 8 weeks; meaning she was able to work without communicating with a peer or the teacher. "I think I'm more successful right now because I'm working alone." Clearly, this student advocated for herself, knew what type of learning environment she needed, and grew because of those choices.

Student 6 and Student 4 made very different choices along the way. Each of these students has struggled in the past with staying on task in the art room. Student 6 made careful choices early on in the 8-week class. He decided to make the most of the online materials and worked out of class. Student 4 worked mainly in class, was a collaborative learner, and only asked for clarification toward the end of the entire 8-week class.

In contrast, Students 7 and 1, with two very different learning styles, were both able to demonstrate high levels of independent learning throughout the 8 weeks. Student 7 was a dependent learner at first and then quickly switched to an independent learning style. He chose to use communication for clarification purposes only. This student determined quickly that collaboration was not a helpful learning style in achieving and chose to communicate with the teacher only after the first week. When asked about his learning style and how he stays motivated, he replied, "I was independent throughout the whole thing and I watched videos on my own and tried to get things done myself. I think I'm more successful right now because I don't have people around me I can talk to that will distract me."

Student 1 was able to use collaboration as a stepping stone to develop independent skills and habits. The last half of the class (Weeks 5–8) this student became comfortable with working alone. This flipped method provided a flexible platform so students could learn how to be an engaged learner. They learned to change learning styles, make personal choices, become responsible, and take risks.

Not all students had the same struggles and some even began to ask questions about new ideas. Student 8 stated, "My learning style did change when I started to work before class or started to watch videos before class. Then I was able to work more during class."

In this way, each student had to learn how to manage their time and needed to make the most of every opportunity in class. Many students stated that they wanted to "be prepared for class" so they had more "time to ask questions and do their best" on their project. Students also became aware of the space around them. They began asking to be moved away from certain individuals; they decided to talk less or collaborate more to be productive.

**Engagement: Investment and Motivation**

Students showed motivation in their time, effort, and reflective qualities; they had a drive to continue working. Student 8 is perfect example of students becoming invested in their work. As students answered required reflection questions, they began to think, ask, and reflect honestly without prompts; they made personal goals and choices on their own. Students made changes in their learning path that made them more focused, and in turn they became invested in their learning experience. One student stated, "I became more independent throughout the projects and my motivation improved as well. I started to ask questions or ask for help at the beginning."

There were many ways students became motivated throughout the 8 weeks. I observed students advocating for themselves, changing their daily work habits (in class and out of class), and taking risks. From a bird's-eye view, Students 1, 2, and 3 revealed personal changes that removed distractions and allowed each student to become more engaged in their own learning.

Several of these students were more collaborative at the beginning of the 8 weeks. As the class progressed, they learned they would have to change their learning style to be productive as the flipped method requires students to be independent. All students developed a need for working outside the classroom. Some decided to be prepared before class started. Others watched tutorials and took their project home. These choices became a habit for many students; it just happened in a different time frame for each student.

**Self-Reflection and Resilience**

Editing and reflection are natural parts of the art process, but students had to learn to self-advocate and find motivation to reflect and grow. I embedded a set of graded reflective questions at different stages as each project progressed. The interesting finding is that students took it one step farther in their experience. Many students began writing out personal goals. As an example, students were expected to reflect and evaluate their projects; this routine has been in place since 6th grade. One student indicated he wrote a personal goal two times. He felt the need to reflect more in addition to the required class reflections.

Many of the personal goals that students wrote down were about talking less, not getting distracted, and being able to work faster in class. Student 2 wrote, "I need to be more focused on my work." Because this method provides an opportunity for students to work at their own pace, students made personal goals that impacted their learning directly. One week after Student 2 wrote that personal goal, his focus in class was completely independent.

Students practiced resilience (the ability to recover and adapt to difficulties) and self-efficacy throughout the 8 weeks. Self-efficacy refers to confidence or a personal belief of a desired outcome (Bandura, 1989; LaMorte, 2019). Through my research, I found students gained both attributes through reflective practice and teacher support. One student shared this insight with me, "I've worked with art before, and it can be really frustrating at times. You may make plenty of mistakes, but usually the end is almost always worth it. If it isn't, well at least you attempted something new." As this student simply implied, resilient students learned simply by trying, revising, and reflecting; they didn't give up. It doesn't mean students should be perfect; it means they should feel accomplishment in their hard work and effort. As students became more confident, they showed more interest in their choices and felt ownership in their actions. As an example, Student 7 finally took ownership in his choices. He advocated, showed resilience, and developed self-efficacy over these 8 weeks. Critically self-assessing his skills through reflection, student collaboration, and asking clarifying questions became a habit. Student 7 began the course as a dependent student (which I have observed over the prior 2 years). As he moved forward on his learning path, he became more independent through advocating and collaborating with others. Communication was the bridge for this student to begin working independently in and out of the classroom. The more Student 7 became comfortable asking questions, the more he would reflect, work outside of class, and show a motivated and invested effort by taking risks and owning his decision-making. In turn, this student developed self-efficacy.

## CONCLUSIONS

At the end of the 8 weeks, findings suggest that when projects scaffolded to build habits and skills towards resilience and self-efficacy (key student attributes) were combined with teacher support, students' independent learning increased. Each student observed and then adapted daily outcomes. They returned, engaged, asked questions, collaborated, reflected, and edited; proof that Bandura's (1989) social cognitive theory works. I found that each of the prior skills were on a continuum. Students self-advocated through communication first. Then the findings revealed they were in control of clarification, collaboration, their art process, and reflection.

The art room is a perfect place for students to become independent through the flipped classroom model. Students can individualize their own path and take ownership of their learning. In return, this method motivates students to become engaged learners and find their voice. If used in combination with self-reflection, the flipped method can help students develop resilience and self-efficacy. The flipped method gives students the flexibility to grow as well as allows teachers to meet all student needs within the classroom. Based on these findings, I can conclude that this experience in flipped teaching is truly a positive experience for my students. Teachers have the opportunity to deliver instruction multiple ways, and students can learn at their own pace no matter their skill level. Both the teacher and student are crucial and have a part to play as students become invested and take ownership in their learning.

This study on the flipped method provides evidence that students need an environment in which they can practice advocating for themselves as well as reminders to pause and reflect; students must look back at how far they have come. Only then will a student see worth in their invested time, show self-efficacy, find resilience, and truly become an independent learner. These skills and habits allow students to further their education without the teacher. Understanding that they have the adaptive skills and the knowledge to make mistakes and yet persevere provides the needed confidence to navigate high school difficulties and life outside K–12 education.

In light of the COVID-19 pandemic, education has changed and will continue to evolve. Educators can no longer expect to teach students without giving them online opportunities. This flipped classroom method allows all teachers the ability to plan for students in and out of the school setting, save planning time through district learning management systems, and expand the world of education and 21st-century learning. As art teachers, we can strive to teach our students ownership and empowerment through problem-solving, independence, and responsibility within this chaotic yet productive environment.

## REFERENCES

Bandura, A. (1989). Social cognitive theory. In R. Vasta (Ed.), *Annals of child development* (Vol. 6), *Six theories of child development* (pp. 1–60). JAI Press.

Bergmann, J., & Sams, A. (2012). *Flip your classroom: Reach every student in every class every day*. International Society for Technology in Education.

Cheng, L., Ritzhaupt, A. D., & Antonenko, P. (2018). Effects of the flipped classroom instructional strategy on students' learning outcomes: A meta-analysis. *Educational Technology Research and Development, 67*(4), 793–824. https://doi.org/10.1007/s11423-018-9633-7

Delacruz, E. M. (2009). Art education aims in the age of New Media: Moving toward global civil society. *Art Education, 62*(5), 13–18. https://doi.org/10.1080/00043125.2009.11519032

Fulton, K. P. (2012). 10 reasons to flip. *Phi Delta Kappan, 94*(2), 20–24. https://doi.org/10.1177/003172171209400205

Hopper, J. J. (2016). Digitizing the easel: Student perspectives on tutorial videos in the art classroom. *Art Education, 69*(4), 23–28. https://doi.org/10.1080/00043125.2016.1176487

Iowa Core. (n.d.a). *Employability Skills*. Retrieved May 4, 2020, from https://educateiowa.gov/standard/21st-century-skills/employability-skills-21st-century-skills

Iowa Core. (n.d.b). *Technology Literacy*. Retrieved May 4, 2020, from https://educateiowa.gov/standard/21st-century-skills/technology-literacy-21st-century-skills

Iowa Department of Education. (2020). Data and Reporting. Retrieved August 16, 2020, from https://educateiowa.gov/data-reporting/data-and-reporting

Lage, M. J., Platt, G. J., & Treglia, M. (2000). Inverting the classroom: A gateway to creating an inclusive learning environment. *The Journal of Economic Education, 31*(1), 30–43. https://doi.org/10.2307/1183338

LaMorte, W. W. (2019). *Behavioral Change Models*. Retrieved August 16, 2020, from https://sphweb.bumc.bu.edu/otlt/MPH-Modules/SB/BehavioralChangeTheories/BehavioralChangeTheories5.html

Morgan, H. (2014). Focus on technology: Flip your classroom to increase academic achievement. *Childhood Education, 90*(3), 239–241. https://doi.org/10.1080/00094056.2014.912076

Roehl, A., Reddy, S. L., & Shannon, G. J. (2013). The flipped classroom: An opportunity to engage millennial students through active learning strategies. *Journal of Family & Consumer Sciences, 105*(2), 44–49. https://doi.org/10.14307/JFCS105.2.12

Roehling, P. V., Luna, L. M., Richie, F. J., & Shaughnessy, J. J. (2017). The benefits, drawbacks, and challenges of using the flipped classroom in an introduction to psychology course. *Teaching of Psychology, 44*(3), 183–192. https://doi.org/10.1177/0098628317711282

Varier, D., Dumke, E. K., Abrams, L. M., Conklin, S. B., Barnes, J. S., & Hoover, N. R. (2017). Potential of one-to-one technologies in the classroom: Teachers and students weigh in. *Educational Technology Research and Development, 65*(4), 967–992. https://doi.org/10.1007/s11423-017-9509-2

# Part II

# NURTURING SELF-EFFICACY AND VOICE

*Samantha Goss*

According to Dewey (1916), a democratic way of life welcomes expressions of difference, which can add to everyone's life experiences. Members of a democracy find shared interests and concerns across their multiple voices and use their personal capacities to continually evolve society in beneficial ways. In the previous chapter, the importance of student choice and ways to empower students to make impactful choices were presented. Democratic society provides the freedom of choice, which must be practiced and guided through education (Dewey, 1916). Making a choice is an expression of individual voice, which connects the next set of chapters. A multitude of voices are necessary in a democracy. Expressing voice not only gives importance to the speaker but also provides opportunities to grow from perspective taking (Perkins & Carter, 2011; Shields et al., 2020). Finding voice and hearing other voices are essential parts, but in addition, each individual and the democratic society must use voice for change.

A democratic culture that welcomes all voices is vitally important to correct and resist the patterns of marginalization and silencing that have historically existed in our society. It becomes even more important to teach developing citizens how to express and listen to voice. Expression, however, is not a guarantee that others will have a shared experience. Gude (2009) reminds us that democratic life requires each of us to be able to remain an individual and part of the collective, even when we are alone in our identity. Some isolation is to be expected but should not equate to silence or erasure. Desai (2020) stressed the importance of the visual arts for illuminating those made invisible, or erased, and making change. Through making and viewing art, and receiving another's voice, art educators can mentor students in how to question what they see and what has been hidden in order to see, hear, and critically reflect on a whole picture. Here, voice and visuals support the inclusion and progress of democracy.

Gude (2009) advocates for the many ways that art education supports voice and the multiplicity of voices necessary for democracy. Through curriculum and assessments, art educators convey their values for learning (Hogan et al., 2020). This message has implications beyond the art classroom if we consider Dewey's belief that all education prepares students for democratic life. The responsibility of the art educator is to consider opportunities for voice in the incorporation of student experiences as content or their unique paths to expression (Gude, 2009). Finally, the role of voice in societal dialogue and its possible impact should be guided and practiced through quality art education.

In Chapter 4, Heather Walker describes how using art journaling and Studio Habits of Mind can support the personal connections and meaning that communicate student voice. Hetland et al.'s (2013) Studio Habits of Mind are dispositions that are important for engaging in art. These beliefs, attitudes, and habits relate to the habits of mind Dewey (1916) found critically important for democracy. In both, students must be taught and encouraged to engage with these habits of mind. Reflection allows students to better perceive a context and possibly hear others' voices. Later, voice comes through as students express their meaning. Walker's research values a growth mindset, or a focus on the personal capabilities students can develop that Dewey saw as important contributions to our democratic society. The Friday activities in this study reflect the importance of not only sharing one's voice but also valuing those of others through the exploration of new art and artists.

Teachers must make the decision to foster democracy in their own classrooms, and in Chapter 5, Maddison Maddock notices a lack of voice and opportunities for voice in her classroom. To address this, she worked with an elementary art club to promote the arts. While her position influenced the general context, within the club, students were given opportunities to learn how to use their voices in collaboration with others. Their shared goals were a club name and a community event to promote the arts, though each individual contributed based on their interests and strengths. In line with Dewey's beliefs, Maddock guided their development by prompting their need for a purpose and explaining how to productively communicate. She took the lead on teaching the necessary skills, but the students' voices directed the rest of the experience. Based on postsurveys, students evolved from believing that using their voices meant literally to talk, to understanding this could mean contributing ideas, listening, and taking action.

In the previous chapters, students found their voices and experienced the impact they can have in their community, whether in an art class or club. In Chapter 6, Jodi Fenton considers types of reflection and their impact on students' voices, specifically regarding self-efficacy. As evidenced throughout this book, reflection is essential for clarifying the message voiced, understanding the greater context beyond oneself, and considering how to take action or effect change. While reflection was the shared interest of the whole class, different individuals preferred specific methods of reflection, as is the case in society. Ultimately, Fenton shows that, in achieving the shared goal of reflection, students should be provided with choice that reflects their autonomy. Self-efficacy is beneficial for all students but even more important when fighting a culture of invisibility (Desai, 2020). Self-efficacy and students' voices could increase with productive reflection through a variety of methods.

## REFERENCES

Desai, D. (2020). Educating for social change through art: A personal reckoning. *Studies in Art Education, 61*(1), 10–23.

Dewey, J. (1916). *Democracy and education: An introduction to the philosophy of education.* The Free Press.

Gude, O. (2009). The 2009 Lowenfeld Lecture: Art education for democratic life. *Studies in Art Education, 62*(6), 6–11.

Hetland, L., Winner, E., Veenema, S., & Sheridan, K. M. (2013). *Studio thinking 2: The real benefits of visual arts education* (2nd ed.). Teachers College Press.

Hogan, J., Jacquith, D., & Gould, L. (2020). Shifting perceptions of quality in art education. *Art Education, 73*(4), 8–13.

Perkins, E. G., & Carter, M. C. (2011). In search of the wild things: The choice, voice, and challenge (CVC) model for creative instruction. *Art Education, 64*(1), 20–24.

Shields, S. S., Fendler, R., & Henn, D. (2020). A vision of civically engaged art education: Teens as arts-based researchers. *Studies in Art Education, 61*(2), 123–141.

CHAPTER 4

# How Art Journaling and Studio Habits of Mind Encourage Personal Connections in High School Student Art Making

*Heather Walker*

Imagine you just delivered an introduction to a new project. You were excited, animated, and your classroom management was flawless. The project includes ample amounts of scaffolding, skill building, differentiation, and student choice. You are confident the students are going to produce amazing, authentic original artwork! You imagine the possibilities and artwork hanging on the wall. Then you hear: "I am not creative." "I do not have any imagination." "I can't even draw a stick figure." "A shoe has more artistic ability than I do." "I do not know what to draw." "I have zero ideas." "Can I just copy this thing I saw on Pinterest?" Your heart sinks. The students have barely started, and it seems they are already giving up.

Art is one way of expressing an individual's emotions, thoughts, and personal experiences. One of the first things humans learn is how to create marks on paper. This is my definition of an *artist*. The challenge is remaining an artist as we grow up. At what point do individuals stop making art about their emotions, experiences, and thoughts? What stops people from continuing to create? In the field of art, Viktor Lowenfeld's six stages of artistic development provide a foundational outline for how artistic skills originate and grow (Lowenfeld & Brittain, 1987).

One of Lowenfeld's most critical findings is the description of the sixth and final stage of artistic development called the *Decision Stage* (Lowenfeld & Brittain, 1987). During the *Decision Stage* (usually 8th grade to about sophomore year in high school), levels of self-criticism are at an all-time high. Many people believe drawing is a skill they do not possess and will simply stop creating altogether. Others will continue to practice their skills and work through challenges. When actually making artwork, some students struggle to be engaged, come up with creative ideas, and work through challenges. With all this student variety, what can art teachers do to make art relevant, personal, enjoyable, and engaging?

In the art room, self-perception of artistic ability is often a challenging obstacle. We need students to be able to see themselves as efficacious in art, as in all areas of life, to function as a deliberative, creative society. What can I do as an artist and teacher to help students overcome these challenges? How can I help students to think and act like artists? How can students be motivated to develop more creative ideas and make more personally meaningful artwork?

Student engagement and motivation are persistent challenges in all areas of education, and multiple efforts to influence these topics have been examined. However, specifically for art education, the research is lacking a deeper understanding of how teachers can help student artists *develop* motivation, habits for success, and methods to foster personal relevance in art. In a pivotal study conducted through Harvard University's Project Zero, researchers Hetland, Winner, Veenema, and Sheridan (2013) addressed the hidden curriculum of art classes that they called the Studio Habits of the Mind (or Studio Habits for short). As the researchers observed three art programs, they identified and examined eight habits: Develop Craft, Engage & Persist, Envision, Express, Observe, Reflect, Stretch & Explore, and Understand Art Worlds. Since the publication of this study, additional research has taken place on the integration of these Studio Habits into schools. In 2015, five middle schools in Oregon adopted a program called ArtCore. This program's focus was the integration of the Studio Habits into their whole school curriculum (Anderson, 2015). As I pondered the artistic obstacles in my classroom, I asked myself: What would happen if the Studio Habits were not a hidden curriculum that art teachers hoped students noticed along the way but instead were explicitly taught to students? How would students react if they were taught the importance of these artistic habits and were invited to experience the habits by making art and reflecting in artist journals? If I could invite them to discover art in the world around them and within their personal worlds, maybe that would make a difference in how students perceived their own artistic abilities and connections to art.

More specifically, I wanted to discover and describe the ways in which the eight Studio Habits of Mind, combined with visual art journaling, impacted three art classes I teach in a high school with grades 9–12. This school had a student population of 298 (144 males and 154 females); 36 percent qualified for free or reduced lunch. Demographics of the student body were as follows: 75 percent identified as White; 22 percent as Hispanic; and less than 1 percent as Black or two or more races. A total of 30 participants (24 female and 6 male) engaged in my study. Their grade levels ranged from 9 to 12, and ages from 14 to 18.

## INTRODUCING CREATIVE AND REFLECTIVE ACTIVITIES

The central questions of my study were:

- How can students be motivated to develop more creative ideas and make more personally meaningful artwork?
- How do skill building, art medium experimentation, failure, and play contribute to a student's performance and growth in an art class?

I planned the creative and reflective activities in this research in a way that would encourage participants to shape their own knowledge and conclusions. I anticipated that the Studio Habits of Mind combined with art journaling would foster personal connections, motivate students, lead to better quality and personally meaningful artworks, and encourage students' regular use of the Studio Habits. The interaction with the Studio Habits would then transition into permanent skills also affecting other content areas and continue to strengthen as students progress through the semester.

As an artist, I strongly believe in the value of practice to build skills and techniques. Traditionally, I had students emulate artistic practice by requiring them to create weekly sketchbook drawings. I had seen students struggle to complete and make original and creative artworks in their sketchbooks. As a graduate student, I studied art journaling, a process that would encourage students to reflect while creating and would help foster personal connections to their work. I incorporated this journaling process into my study as a strategy through sketchbooks and students' digital portfolios.

I conducted my research over the course of 16 weeks in three art classes: Art 1 (Beginner), Art 2 (Intermediate), and Independent Studio (Advanced). I collected data from activities that took place in the three art classes on Fridays. The activities included art journaling, creative bank account building, responding to reflection questions, and creating sketchbooks, which were called Art Medium Mayhems. My data also included field notes, photographs, pre- and post-surveys, and student responses using an app called Kaizena.

I began by giving student participants an anonymous pre-study survey on Google Forms to complete during class time. The goal of this survey was to gauge students' perceptions, attitudes, beliefs about art, reasons for taking the class, and motivation levels. This was followed by a postsurvey after the project concluded.

All students in art classes are required to keep a digital portfolio by photographing the artwork they create over the course of 4 years at high school. These portfolios serve as a record of their growth through their art classes. For my study, portfolios were modified and utilized as a way for students to journal, record reflections, and organize their knowledge. Students created their portfolios using a Google Slides presentation. Each week on Friday, portfolios were updated by students with the week's activities. Within these portfolios, students answered reflection questions about the Studio Habit they studied and the artwork they created. It was a powerful reflection tool because it served as a digital record of student growth.

The art-journaling activity on Fridays began with activity instructions and a short video about the Studio Habit of the week. Students were asked to reflect through open-ended questions after each video, such as what the habit meant, an example of a time they employed the habit, and why the habit was important to exhibit. Each week the questions varied slightly to best fit the Studio Habit and the types of data collected. All student responses to these questions were recorded in the student's individual digital portfolio. It was my hope that art journaling would instill the habit in the students' minds and inspire them to exhibit the habit. In addition, I hoped that the student would become aware of how artists utilized the habit of reflective journaling to be successful.

Another strategy I used with students was creative bank accounts. During art-journaling Fridays, after students had completed their journal reflections about the Studio Habit of the week, they were asked to discover and explore contemporary artists that inspired them. To introduce this concept at the beginning of the study, students viewed a short YouTube video entitled "Your Creative Bank Account" by the artist Jake Parker (2016). This video emphasizes the importance of surrounding oneself with visual inspiration because without inspiration, our creative bank accounts become empty, and one cannot draw from an empty bank account. The goal of this strategy was to help students become inspired by contemporary artists with the hope that creating projects or sketchbooks would become easier and more engaging after making connections to those artists. Students concluded each journal entry by adding a new slide in their digital portfolio with the artist's name, two pictures of the artist's work, and a description as to why they chose that artist or how they were inspired by the artist. I included this activity so that students would see that art was real and alive in today's world. I gave students a list of websites they could use and encouraged them to discover others on their own. Through finding artists to inspire them, students saw that art can be created with any material and about any topic they were interested in. This also added an element of choice to the study that gave students freedom and autonomy to choose artists who inspired them and were linked to their interests.

Friday activities alternated between art journaling and sketchbooks called Art Medium Mayhems. For Art Medium Mayhems, students began by watching a short video I prepared that recapped the previous week and the Studio Habit being explored. In the recap video, I informed students what their art journal reflections revealed from the previous week and determined what the meaning of the Studio Habit was. In the "Mayhems" students were encouraged to try new art mediums and create a sketch in

How Art Journaling and Studio Habits of Mind Encourage Connections    71

**Figure 4.1. An example of an Art Medium Mayhem screenshot of student's digital portfolio reflection from student participant ART2A**

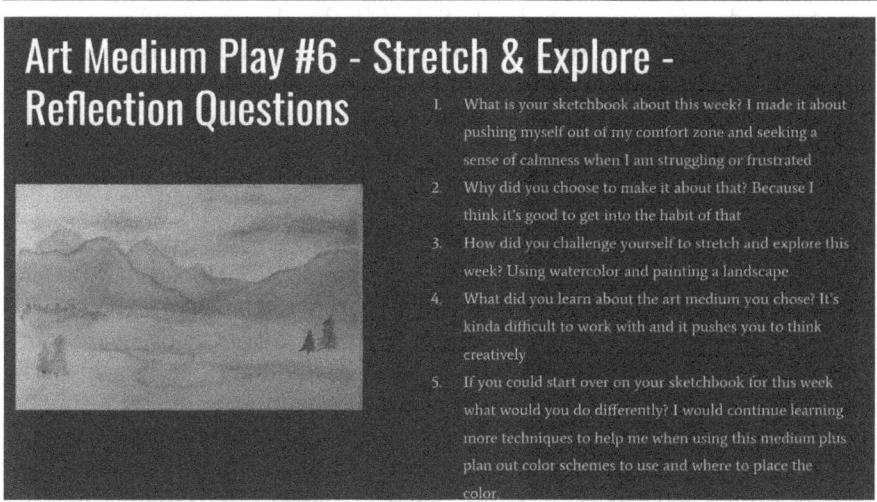

their journals that was connected to their personal interests or was inspired by the artist they chose the previous week. For some Studio Habits, students were asked to do something specifically linked to practicing that habit. For example, in the week of the Studio Habit "Observe," they picked a small object from a box to observe and draw in their sketchbooks. Most weeks were planned to keep the sketchbooks as open-ended as possible while still related to the Studio Habit of the week. Students were able to use around 20–25 minutes of class time to work in their sketchbooks creating their artwork. They were required to turn in their artwork on Monday so I could examine it. Students photographed each sketch and added them to their digital portfolios. They also answered specific reflection questions about the creation of the sketchbooks within their portfolios (Figure 4.1). These reflection questions encompassed what art medium they worked with, what they learned, what they made, and why. In art classes prior to this study, students were required to create weekly sketchbook drawings, but to enhance the curriculum in my research, a meaningful purpose and focus was given to the sketches, which included room for student exploration, failure, opportunity for them to make personal art, time in class to create their sketches, and opportunities to practice the Studio Habit of the week.

## ANALYZING STUDENT GROWTH IN ART CLASS

Following the 16 weeks of my action research, I analyzed the data I had collected and will share my conclusions in the following sections.

## Motivation and Mindset

Mindset and motivation are closely linked in the classroom. If students do not have a positive mindset or do not believe they can do a task, they may start with a negative mindset and be unmotivated to create (Dweck, 2016). In my pre-study survey mentioned earlier, students were asked, "On a scale of 1 to 10, how do you feel about taking an art class?" The 1 on the scale represented "not excited at all, I don't want to be here," 5 meant "I am okay with being here," and 10 represented "I am extremely excited to be here." The responses to this question showed 17 of the 30 participants gave a ranking of 10, and no students selected a ranking less than 5. I concluded that the majority of students were motivated to take the art class they had signed up for.

These results indicated that within the participants, most were motivated to be in the class already. Participants were additionally asked why they chose to take the art class they selected. The most common responses included interest in art from prior experience, desire to improve/grow, art was a way to be creative and fun, and to express oneself. Less common responses included a previously established relationship to the teacher and a feeling of safety. Out of the 30 participants, only one student indicated being placed in the class by the counselor.

Students were also asked to rank their art skills or abilities on a scale of 1 to 10, with 10 indicating student self-perception of ability as high; 5, as average; and 0 as poor. The results of this question varied. The majority ranked themselves from a 5 to an 8 in art skill. This revealed that most students ranked themselves with average skill or slightly above and corresponds with student self-selection for the class. Five students ranked themselves with below-average art ability.

The last survey question assessed student perception of access to and value of the arts. Students were asked to respond to this statement: "Anyone can become an artist; anyone can make art." This question was a way of asking how much they believed in themselves to become artists and their interest or value in the arts. Eighteen students stated they strongly agreed, nine agreed, two neither agreed nor disagreed, one student disagreed, and zero strongly disagreed. The one participant who disagreed elected to explain why and said, "I disagree, but I want to explain why. I disagree because I don't think everyone has the will and drive to keep practicing enough to try to be better." This specific response demonstrates the link between motivation and mindset. It reinforced the claims from the literature review that, without the right mindset, the ability and desire to create are absent (Potter & Edens, 2001). These results suggest that the majority of student participants started out with a growth mindset at the beginning of the study and wanted to be in the class.

As I explained earlier, every week students answered open-ended questions and reflected on the habit of the week in their digital portfolios.

They created artwork and experimented with art mediums in their sketchbooks. A common theme in student responses across each Studio Habit was that in order to improve their art skills, it was necessary to practice and exhibit the habit of the week. Students acknowledged that each Studio Habit had its own individual strengths and purpose. Studio Habits contributed positively to student motivation in class. Students' portfolio responses indicated they discovered the link between Studio Habits and success and that practicing these habits would lead to improved skills. This realization of the habits they encountered contributed to their motivation and mindset in order to be successful artists and individuals.

Throughout the six samples I examined, students demonstrated awareness of the critical role Studio Habits played (Table 4.1). All six students' individual responses included statements indicating their desire to improve their art, to make things look correct and accurate, to convey emotions, and to evaluate oneself as a way to improve. Students exhibited positive attitudes toward the Studio Habits over the course of the study, and no student response ever indicated that a habit was not important or had no purpose. Every week students were able to connect and reflect upon why the habit would be essential to exhibit. Through Art Medium Mayhems (sketchbooks), students practiced how that habit worked. Student comments in their digital portfolio reflections revealed that students were motivated when there was some aspect of choice for the week as well as some element of freedom to choose their art's subject matter or art medium.

Creative bank accounts in students' digital portfolios seem to have contributed to their motivation. Students explored the variety of ways art could

**Table 4.1. Student Responses from Digital Portfolios on the Importance of Studio Habits**

| Questions on Studio Habits | Themes and Trends of Student Responses |
|---|---|
| In your own words why is **observing** a good habit important? | Make things more realistic/accurate/detailed |
| | Life skill—applied outside of art—friendships, jobs, other subjects |
| | Notice things—awareness—appreciate details |
| In your own words why is **expressing** a good habit important? | A healthy vent of emotions |
| | A way to connect with others / relate to others |
| | A way to send a message / communicate in your art |
| In your own words why is **reflecting** a good habit important? | A way to look at strengths and weaknesses |
| | To help you grow, learn, understand, improve your art |
| | "If you can't reflect, you can't improve." —Student quote |

be created and explored their personal interests by finding artists they appreciated and could connect to. This built on students' abilities to research and analyze information to create personal connections to the world of art.

In my post-study survey I asked students to rank their effort on a scale of 1 to 10. All students gave themselves a score of 6 or higher. The majority of the responses, 14, said they were giving themselves a 9 for effort, seven participants said 10, and six said 8. This revealed that students were still engaged in the activities on Friday and giving their best effort. I was concerned that midway through the study, students would become disinterested in the activities and stop seeing the purpose. However, this survey's results suggest that these groups of students were still motivated in the class, had seen personal growth, and valued the activities on Fridays.

Lastly, the post-study survey asked if students saw growth when looking back at their digital portfolios as the class progressed. Twenty-seven participants said yes, and three said they had seen no personal growth in their digital portfolios. All six student samples stated that they had seen growth over the semester in their digital portfolios.

**Demonstration of Studio Habits**

I used the Studio Habits of Mind to guide student exploration, reflection, and learning. The pre-study survey provided insight into what habits students already exhibited along with their current approaches and attitudes towards making art. Participants were asked, "What makes a work of art good?" Common responses suggested that students believed that art needed to be original and detailed. It should have meaning and reflect the artist's effort and time spent working on it. Students thought its quality was based on how the artist felt about the creation when it was finished. Students were asked what habits a successful artist displayed. They commonly responded with "practice, perseverance, motivation, creativity, and passion." Students clearly had some ideas at the beginning of the study on what it took to be an artist and how art should be created.

One way for students to find the originality they deemed important may have been through trying new media. In their sketchbooks, Art 1 students' creations showed that they regularly explored new art mediums (Figure 4.2). In fact, they rarely worked with the same medium in their first four sketchbooks. Art 1 students were quick to determine interests and make personal connections to what they wanted to make art about. Art 2 students worked in their interest areas including nature, landscapes, portraits, animals, global issues, or comics. They mostly stuck to similar mediums or focused on mediums that were being used in current class projects or the art mediums they felt most confident with. Independent Studio participants' sketches varied weekly, from working with themes they had selected for the class's duration to exploring different creative techniques.

How Art Journaling and Studio Habits of Mind Encourage Connections        75

**Figure 4.2. Examples of pages from students' sketchbooks**

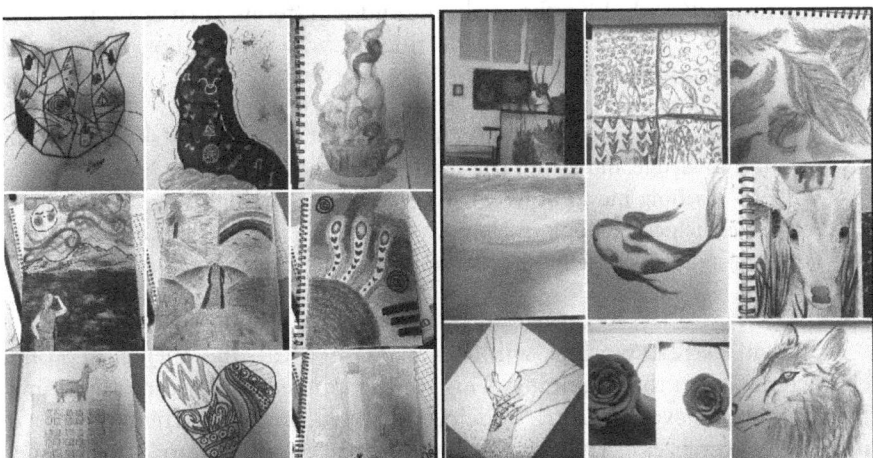

After 8 weeks of participating in the study, students were asked to rate how much they felt they had grown as an artist as a result of working with the Studio Habits. All students stated they displayed growth as an artist.

Closer examination of the six sample participants revealed that the student I designate as Art1A consistently tried new mediums in her sketchbook work. This reflected her willingness to experiment. In the week focused on the Studio Habit "Observe," Art1A reflected as she drew a classroom plant, "I noticed that the plant curved in different ways and the outer edges near the tip were a darker green than the center." At the end of the study, this student ranked her art growth as an 8. Art1A journal reflections on Developing Craft stated, "I have learned new ways to do things by thinking about a project longer and planning it out, rather than just doing something right away." The Observation habit taught the student. "I have learned to look at things longer. I study the details of an object more and notice things that I probably haven't noticed before." The week of Express engaged the student. "It helps me think about my mental state with art. Sometimes I'm not very confident in what I draw or make in art and by reflecting, it helps me think of where the project started and how it changed or looked different by the end."

A student designated as Art1B decided on a theme early in the study and made art about his love of sports. At the end of the study, he ranked his art growth as an 8 and reported

> This class has been so helpful in learning the techniques of art. I honestly think I will learn more this year than all of my other years in art, I was always pretty observant from playing video games but I have now noticed some of the reasons things were there not just what they were. Reflecting has helped when making adjustments and becoming a better artist.

Turning to the Art 2 class, student Art2A rated her growth as a 9. She decided to work with different mediums and in different themes with a focus on art skill development. When reflecting on how the Studio Habits influenced her, student Art2A said

> This class has helped me develop craft by helping me learn new skills to expand my art knowledge and grow. This class has helped me improve my observation skills by teaching me to draw what I see not what I think I see. Practicing to reflect has helped me look over my work and give me the chance to look back at the mistakes I made and how I can improve the next time I put those skills to work.

Student Art2B worked within a passion area—the theme of comic characters—from the beginning. This student ranked his art growth as an 8. He said about Develop Craft, "It helped me by having me learn more skills to use for my art pieces." The Observe habit helped the student to "learn how to really look at an art piece by looking for the finer details." As for Reflecting, he explained, "It helped me by making me look back at what I could have done better about my art and what I can do to improve it in the future."

Both Independent Studio participants ranked their growth as a 10. IndStu1 stated

> Develop Craft helped because I'm grasping more control over mediums and trying new ones also. Observe has improved because I look more at little details and other details as well. It's something we constantly do and Reflect helps me think about how I want to grow as an artist and what I want to do next and improve in.

IndStu2 reflected

> I have gotten to develop craft as an artist to spread out with new materials and got to see how each work with my style. I've grown to take things slow and to take it easy on my art, give it time and give it a chance even if I dislike it. At the moment I'm working on a new project that requires me to observe closer into detail. Like for example, the main focus on my piece is a coyote with flowers. For that, I need to observe and look closer into the details of the animal's fur and the way the flowers look and their color. Lastly, reflect, has helped me want to improve, make my art better than the last one. To grow stronger as an artist.

In sum, I found that the creative and reflective activities I introduced for my research enabled each student to interact deeply with and practice the Studio Habits as demonstrated in the students' quotes. The curriculum modifications allowed students to personally connect to the habits as well as the art they were making, which positively influenced attitudes, behaviors, and growth in the art classroom. Reflection and journaling played a large role in this data collection and understanding how students were affected. By interacting with Studio Habits in multiple ways and reflecting on their decisions and artwork, students were more able to feel connected, motivated, and invested in their artwork.

**Personal Connections**

Personal connections to creating art was a central theme that emerged in this study. Creating personal connections is not always an easy task for teachers to accomplish. We are often so focused on what we are teaching instead of why we are teaching it or how to make it meaningful (Wiggins & McTighe, 2005). This study showed that the more students related to the art they made or the habit they explored, the more invested they became. The pre-study survey gave insight into how students generated ideas for making art and why they created art before the study activities began. This was helpful to know to compare the students' pre-study methods in contrast to the methods and activities that were planned to help students during the study.

Students primarily relied on external influences to make art. Most made art as an outlet. They enjoyed making art about emotions and nature, and they felt they could make art about a variety of topics. Although students referenced looking online for ideas in the pre-study survey, they did not mention that looking at other artists inspired them. Looking at and copying other art was one method they relied on, rather than coming up with their own unique ideas. Students often looked inward to their emotions for inspiration. It was my hope that the study activities would encourage students to make stronger personal connections to art as well as more original and authentic work.

The post-study survey suggests that students were better able to make personal connections to their artwork. Students said that the Friday activities helped them to express themselves, observe more closely, open them up to new kinds of art and artists, build their art skills and techniques, encourage them to try new things, think about art's purpose and meaning, and be inspired. One student responded, "I think the trait I noticed the most is my observation. I notice artwork in places I never would have even thought to look. I'm also noticing other people's emotions more, which ties in with observation and express." This is supported by the types of sketchbooks students created and their written reflections.

A common hurdle for students to make personal connections to their artwork is the feeling that art is irrelevant and does not have meaning or purpose in today's world. Students can easily list their favorite song or singer, but many are not able to name their favorite visual artist or art medium. This study sought to improve personal connection to art through creative bank accounts. Results indicated that creative bank account building on

Art Journal Fridays enabled students to personally connect to art in today's world. Students were asked in the post-study survey how creative bank accounts had affected them. Common responses were "learning all the different ways to make art," "inspiration," "art is everywhere," "it opened my eyes," "more creativity," and "in the wonder of all the possibilities." By finding artists to inspire them, students' eyes and minds were opened to what art could be and what they could make. Art became more than drawing and painting; instead, they were able to make it personal and meaningful.

Two Studio Habits that I presented in the first 8 weeks were "Express" and "Reflect." These two habits fostered strong personal connections to the artwork. During the week of "Express," students were asked to pick an emotion they often felt and create a work of art based on something they wanted to communicate. Students exhibited a variety of emotions, from joy to fear, to depression, to hope, to calm. Not only did students use symbolism in their artwork to show these feelings, but they considered the art medium that would convey the emotion as well. I noted in my observation journal that students during this Friday in Art 2 were completely silent for the duration of the making time in class. They were engrossed with their work and created deeply personal pieces. During the week of "Reflect," students were partnered and conducted interviews to get to know each other and then create a work of art about their partners (Figure 4.3). This forced students out of their comfort zones; they met someone new and created something for someone other than themselves.

Students again had to consider the medium used to communicate their messages and the likes and dislikes of the other person. While it was not

Figure 4.3. Student reflection example from "Reflect" partner artwork

## ART MEDIUM MAYHEM #4 - REFLECT - REFLECTION QUESTIONS

When you were creating this work of art what were you thinking about?

I was thinking of all the things she said she liked or colors that I could use that she liked.

What are you most proud of in this artwork?

I am most proud of trying to fit what I knew she liked as well as incorporate some abstract work because that is what we've been working on lately.

What could you improve in this artwork?

I could improve on adding some thing, as colorful as it is I still feel like something is missing.

What art materials did you use?

I used oil pastels.

personally connected to them, the artwork had meaning, purpose, and an authentic audience. Art pieces from this week were then exchanged with their partners. Students were very uncomfortable with this activity and self-conscious of their artistic abilities; in spite of this, they reflected that making the art for someone else was a different way of thinking and helped them to grow.

Throughout the activities of the study, I worded reflection questions to encourage students to consider what they personally were interested in and how to connect their interests to making art. By examining their reflection digital portfolios, I noticed that my efforts affected students while they were working on regular projects. I observed students to be more careful making decisions when planning out artwork, considering how to convey expressions, making thoughtful choices on what to do with backgrounds, and what art mediums to use.

Creating personal connections to art is one of the most important things we can do as art educators to enable students to feel art is meaningful and purposeful. The techniques and curriculum changes highlighted in the preceding sections helped students foster unique personal connections to art. The activities were more authentic, individualized, and self-fulfilling because students had choice and autonomy. Reducing my role to a guide by providing these opportunities, students were able to make personal connections through the Studio Habits and curriculum activities.

**Technology to Support Student Growth**

The use of digital technology in this study was crucial to its operation and success. Software and platforms included Google Classroom, Google Drive, Google Slides, Quicktime (to record the videos), and Kaizena (to deliver student feedback). My school is 1:1 with MacBook laptops, and students also use digital tools and apps daily; this is a way to connect personally. I delivered weekly artist journals and Art Medium Mayhem instructions to students through short video walkthroughs. Access to the Internet was of critical importance for students to discover artists for their creative bank accounts. Several websites were provided as suggestions for students to use to find contemporary artists. At times, students accessed social media via personal cell phones to discover artists.

The use of video instruction was chosen as a differentiation tool in this study to allow students control of the instructional video at any time; to pause, rewind, rewatch, and access from anywhere. Videos were posted to Google Classroom for students to access each week. This type of pacing allowed students to work individually at their best pace during the 45-minute class period on Friday. The video covered the Studio Habit of the week by guiding students through a short Google Slides presentation, which was teacher created and modified each week. The videos delivered instructions on how to find artists and sketchbooks. Throughout the study, I completed an example portfolio for each week so students could refer to the assignment and see the teacher completing the assignments as an active participant and artist just like they were.

Using YouTube, I selected a variety of artists to connect to the Studio Habit of the week (Table 4.2). This was a way to foster student curiosity and excitement about art as well as broaden student understanding of what art could be, how it could be created, or what materials it was created from. Creative bank accounts fostered student growth using technology by encouraging them to use their research skills to search the Internet for artists meaningful to them.

**Table 4.2. Artist of the Day Record**

| Artist Name | Subject Matter | Art Medium |
|---|---|---|
| **Studio Habit 1: Develop Craft** | | |
| Blake McFarland | Animals and more | Tire sculpture |
| Josie Lewis | Nature | Resin—layers of clay |
| Ethel Stein | Abstract, human figure, colors | Weaving |
| Jane Kim | Scientific illustration, murals | Paint |
| Robin Eley | Portraits—high resolution, hyper realistic | Paint |
| **Studio Habit 2: Observe** | | |
| Tsering Hannaford | Observational painter of portraits and still life | Paint |
| Joshua Smith | Miniature sculpture artist—urban neighborhoods | Wood, paint, dirt, paper, clay, etc. |
| Lee Hyang-Gu<br>Kim Seong-Tae<br>You Young-Chul<br>Choi In-Gyu<br>Jo Se-Yeon | Masters of ceramics (pottery/clay) | Clay (also called ceramics) |
| Brent Eviston | Nature, portraits, figure | Pencil and charcoal |
| Edward Aldrich | Realism, animal portraits and landscapes | Paint |
| Melissa McCracken | Creates abstract art, hears color, has synesthesia | Oil paint |

How Art Journaling and Studio Habits of Mind Encourage Connections        81

| Artist Name | Subject Matter | Art Medium |
|---|---|---|
| Joshua Miels | Mental health multi-colored portraits | Oil paint |
| Zaria Forman | Icebergs; conservation of Earth; climate change | Chalk pastel |
| **Studio Habit 3: Express** | | |
| Omar Hassan | Abstract; boxing painter | Paint |
| Julia Townsend | Abstract; geometric shapes painter | Oil paint |
| Iris Scott | Nature; professional finger painter | Oil paint |
| Dustin Yellin | Human figures trapped in glass; collage | Layers of glass |
| John Bramblitt | Blind portrait and nature artist | Paint |
| Yulia Brodskaya | Nature, portraits, graphic design, and more | Paper quilling/folding |
| **Studio Habit 4: Reflect** | | |
| Leo Greenfield | Fashion designer | Watercolor & ink |
| Kehinde Wiley | Political; African American presence in artwork | Oil paint |
| Anthony Howe | Sculptures that move in the wind, look like "aliens," "jellyfish," etc. | Metal moving sculptures |
| Shamsia Hassani | Afghani women and culture; street artist, graffiti | Spray paint |
| Bruce Riley | Abstract organic forms—blobs | Resin |
| Benjamin Shine | Portraits; human figures; dancers | Tulle and a hot iron |
| **Studio Habit 5: Envision** | | |
| Mr. Doodle | Doodles on everything | Paint; marker |
| Delita Martin | African American women in artwork | Printmaking |
| Joel Sartore | Nature; *National Geographic* photographer | Photography |
| Rob Gonsalves | Nature; people; magical realism; surrealism; optical illusions; fool the eye | Paint |

| Artist Name | Subject Matter | Art Medium |
|---|---|---|
| Elspeth McLean | Mandala, dots, colorful rocks, dotillism | Paint |
| Emilie Desaunay | Tattoo; nature combined with geometric | Tattoo; ink |
| **Studio Habit 6: Stretch and Explore** | | |
| Ali Golzad | People | Cardboard |
| Alexis Fraser | People; nature; celebrities | Lipstick |
| Alexa Meade | Paints on people to look like paintings | Paint |
| Jake Weidemann | Master penman—calligraphy artist | Ink—calligraphy |
| Dale Chihuly | Organic/abstract looking sculptures | Glass |
| Howard Berger | Special effects movie makeup | Paint, latex, foam rubber, make up |
| Bradley Hart | Portraits; re-creation of famous artworks | Bubble wrap & paint |
| **Studio Habit 7: Engage and Persist** | | |
| Bradley Hart | Mostly re-creates famous paintings | Bubble wrap artist—injects paint into bubble wrap |
| Lisa King | Women; nature; figures | Mural painter |
| Zuly Sanguino | Nature | Artist without limbs—painter |
| Alex Pardee | Graphic design; logos; Hurley graphics designer—skateboards | Paint and digital computer art |
| Emanuele Dascanio | Portraits; flowers, nature | Hyperrealist—super realistic art |
| Edouard Martinet | Bugs and insects—nature | Sculpts bugs from scrap metal |
| **Artist Studio 8: Understand Art Worlds** | | |
| Harriet Riddell | Sewing—portraits/stories | Fabric |
| Peter Drew | Political street artist | Printmaker/signs |
| Flora Bowley | Abstract/free painter | Paint |

| Artist Name | Subject Matter | Art Medium |
| --- | --- | --- |
| Christine Kim | Pattern/geometric portraits | Paper sculpture and drawing |
| Melanie Norris | "Beautiful" portraits | Paint—watercolor and oils |
| Hy Snell, 94 years old | Variety, mostly abstract | Paint |

Kaizena, a web-based application that provides a platform for individual chat, enabled students to turn in their links to their digital portfolios and receive personalized feedback and comments from me about their sketchbook work and journals. This allowed and encouraged a professional teacher–student relationship to form and demonstrated to students that their work mattered and was being thoroughly read and commented on each week. Feedback provided students with validation and encouragement, which continued to promote a motivated student mentality.

## CONCLUSIONS

The primary goal of my study was to determine how specific curriculum changes and utilizing the Studio Habits of Mind would influence students. The curriculum changes were found to positively impact their mindsets, motivation, growth, and ability to make personal connections to art. Students made personal connections to create artwork that was tied to their personal interests or experiences. I found that the pedagogical strategies of art journaling, creative bank account building, artist-of-the-day videos, digital portfolios, student feedback, and Art Medium Mayhems (sketchbooks) are successful tools teachers can use to help students grow artistically, make personal connections, and demonstrate motivation. Students were able to see the relevance and importance of the activities to individual growth.

Motivation and mindset were strongly influenced by allowing the students to build something personal (digital portfolios) and explore their own interests (creative bank accounts and Art Medium Mayhems). The Studio Habits of Mind provided direction and scaffolding to the activities that gave students foundational knowledge to build on. A combination of reflections paired with sketchbooks allowed them to explore Studio Habits in multiple ways. Through creating sketchbooks and trying new art mediums, students were given autonomy and choice. They were able to take risks without the pressure of perfection. Finally, by giving students time in class, they were able to ask questions and complete the activities with guidance from the teacher (Frey & Fisher, 2010). By selecting Studio Habits as a lens of focus, sketchbooks were given a deeper, more meaningful purpose. Students' motivation and mindset were positively impacted as they were able to learn and practice what it meant to think and act as artists.

Personal connections positively impacted student motivation and mindset because art felt personally relevant to the participants. As they discovered contemporary artists in their art journals and portfolios, their minds were opened to the possibilities art has to offer. Their mindsets shifted to realize art was something they were capable of doing. Through being exposed to a variety of artists working with many different materials, they were able to redefine what art meant to them. This implies that it is our job as art educators to expose students to art in today's world and let them discover through their own lenses, not ours.

## REFERENCES

Anderson, R. (2015). *ArtCore Learning Organization*. Retrieved November 28, 2018, from http://www.artcorelearning.org/

Dweck, C. (2016). *Mindset: The new psychology of success*. Random House.

Frey, N., & Fisher, D. (2010). Motivation requires a meaningful task. *The English Journal, 100*(1), 30–36.

Hetland, L., Winner, E., Veenema, S. A., & Sheridan, K. (2013). *Studio thinking 2: The real benefits of visual arts education* (2nd ed.). Teachers College Press.

Lowenfeld, V., & Brittain, W. L. (1987). *Creative and mental growth* (8th ed.). Macmillan.

Parker, J. (2016, September 16). *Your creative bank account* [Video]. YouTube. Retrieved from https://www.youtube.com/watch?v=46OCXFVqRg4

Potter, E. F., & Edens, K. M. (2001). *Children's motivational beliefs about art: Exploring age differences and relation to drawing behavior*. Paper presented at the Annual Meeting of the American Educational Research Association (Seattle, WA, April 10–14, 2001).

Wiggins, G. P., & McTighe, J. (2005). *Understanding by design* (2nd ed.). Association for Supervision and Curriculum Development.

CHAPTER 5

# Enhancing Elementary Student Voice Through Art and Advocacy

*Maddison O. Maddock*

On November 20th, 1989, humans around the world joined together to take a stand on protecting children. Banding together, countries across the globe engaged in writing the Convention on the Rights of the Child, a document that promotes the overall safety of the world's youth and that protects their basic human rights (Lundy, 2007). Over the subsequent years, countries took steps to sign and ratify the Convention, with Somalia being the most recent country to ratify, in 2015. The Convention has become the most widely ratified human rights treaty to date, with nations working together to prioritize the voices and well-being of their young—that is, all nations but one.

The United States, while an active party to drafting the treaty, has yet to ratify the Convention and legally adopt the policies detailed within it. Political opposition and the prioritization of other issues have derailed the ratification. Multiple presidents have referenced the neglect of the Convention, with President Obama declaring it "an embarrassment" that the United States had not yet ratified the treaty (United States: Is Obama's Win . . ., 2008). By failing to do so, the United States has actively denied children the opportunity to be recognized as members of human society with equal rights in many fields, including in Article 12 the right to be given opportunities to express views to those in power and for those opinions to be given due weight and consideration (Lundy, 2007).

Educators work with students who, at times, have difficulty expressing or articulating thoughts or feelings in appropriate ways. Students often share their frustration at not having a space to vocalize how they feel or what they want to communicate. This may be because elementary students, in particular, are rarely viewed as contributors to our society and as citizens that have voices of their own. These young children may not realize the power that they hold in the development of the world's future. Elementary-age students are typically taught to obey adults and to speak when spoken to. Often, student voice is silenced in favor of letting the teacher teach. This creates a culture of silence in which students lose power to represent themselves as members of society. With such a focus on student preparedness for standardized state assessments, critical skills such as communication, leadership, and autonomy are cast aside. This makes one wonder about our children's future—is society raising children to have a base of knowledge, but the inability to independently communicate with one another effectively on issues they care about?

I undertook the study described in this chapter to provide opportunities for students to grow their voice through art advocacy and to develop leadership and communication skills that can be built upon throughout their lives. By honing these skills, students can develop as productive members of society and can begin providing unique insights and voices within their communities. In short, by establishing themselves as active citizens and valuable members of society, children can transition from being predominantly consumers to quality contributors within their communities.

The purpose of my research was to discover the effect of engagement in student-directed art advocacy efforts on the development of student voice in a group of 5th-grade students in an after-school art club environment. I sought to answer the following questions:

- How are communication and/or leadership skills present in the development of student voice?
- What is the teacher's role in the development of student voice?
- How much autonomy should students have at the elementary level in their decision-making processes?
- How do artistic processes utilized in art advocacy activities contribute to the development of student voice?
- How can students work to develop individual voice within a group setting?

I focused on the topics of enhancing student agency and power, logistical considerations, ways in which students express their voices, the role art can play in developing advocates, roles of the teacher in a student-centered environment, and ways to facilitate and personalize student connections to social issues.

Although authors such as Lundy (2007), Serriere et al. (2011), and Bryant and Daniels (2008) demonstrate the importance of student voice and the use of the arts to address social issues, there is little to be found on the impact that arts-specific advocacy can have on elementary-aged students. Only Felleman-Fattal (2017) and Prettyman and Gargarella (2013) have offered viewpoints. Felleman-Fattal suggests that the arts can serve as an effective vehicle to study social issues, which connects strongly to the theme of art advocacy. Prettyman and Gargarella detailed efforts of one art program to engage with the surrounding community through the investigation of social issues, to the benefit of all involved. Student choice was an essential skill to explore over the course of my research, as the skill served to develop ownership and a personal connection with the social issues that students explored.

Buffington (2014) examines how art teachers can work to develop that power and voice through attention to curriculum and pedagogy. Buffington considers multiple approaches—giving attention to developing culturally relevant and student-led projects that enhance student motivation and provide students with a level of power and voice typically not seen in traditional art classroom settings. Buffington maintains that teachers must also develop a sociopolitical consciousness, becoming aware of the inequalities that exist within our culture.

What does authentic student voice look like in the classroom? Bryant and Daniels (2008) provide a model for changing the curriculum so I could help students prepare to act on their convictions. The model suggests a time-conscious, student-focused plan for action that allows for the development of student voice, collaboration, and leadership opportunities. In my research plan, I had students formulate their own learning paths. Additionally, the practice of students being organized into groups based on skill and interest level ensured that students remained focused and motivated throughout their experiences.

Serriere, Mitra, and Reed (2011) demonstrate how important it is to remove oneself from the guiding role and step into the position of a facilitator instead. The authors offer an explicit description of what the varying levels of teacher direction look like, which gives one a realistic idea of how to approach various potential service-learning or student-led experiences within the art classroom. While Serrier et al. worked to identify how student voice can be developed through serving the community, Felleman-Fattal (2017) notes that art and literature can be used to engage students in an investigation into social justice issues. This author writes that literature that examines social issues in age-appropriate language can be used to enhance motivation and student interest in social justice. She postulates that educational curricula have transitioned from developing a multiculturalism mindset, in which students learn about other cultures, to a global competence education, through which students become informed citizens of the world. In our changing world, it is imperative that communities work to help students develop as globally conscious citizens. In order to create better environments and societies, students must understand how they relate to one another and the world. They should be able to formulate ideas and connect to social issues on a personal level and understand how to put those ideas into action. It is the duty of teachers to prepare students with the knowledge they will need to lead productive lives, and part of that knowledge should be understanding that they have a voice and how to use that voice. The art classroom provides an ideal environment in which to foster this knowledge and help students develop their voices through leadership and advocacy for issues they care about.

## VOICE THROUGH VISUAL ART

The intent of my study was to explore and develop change to the power structure that exists between elementary-age students and the adults with whom they interact. I recognized a deficit in the opportunities that young students have to utilize their voices in meaningful matters. Upon realizing the power imbalance that existed, I analyzed current teaching strategies and developed modifications to further foster the development of student voice.

I developed my research plan around the theory that student voice, manifesting through the development of communication and leadership skills, could be explored through the visual arts. The exploration was enhanced through the application of various artistic processes toward art advocacy. In an after-school art club, students developed a central goal of hosting a community art-making advocacy event and then utilized the following club meetings to identify and prepare for the event. The objective of these practices was for students to develop skills to help them to grow and challenge the power imbalances that exist between youth and older generations. The arts can naturally serve as a conduit for the expression of ideas, and art advocacy provided the ideal means to help students be heard (Soundy, 2012). My research examined how power struggles of elementary students can be recognized and challenged by both students and adults through the visual arts, with the hope that the accumulated knowledge from the study will influence future change in perceptions and teaching strategies.

As this study developed, a central focus of developing and empowering students as leaders emerged. Arts advocacy activities facilitated by me, but developed wholly by students, served as opportunities for communication and decision-making skills to be developed.

Participants in my study included nine 5th-grade students who engaged in an after-school art club. The club met once a week over the course of 9 weeks, with the final meeting culminating in an evening community art-making event coordinated and hosted by the participants. The study was conducted at a midwestern suburban public elementary school, which is one of four elementary schools within a rapidly growing district. Eight girls and one boy took part in the study, with all participants identifying as White and not enrolled in any supportive services. This deviates from the demographics of the school as a whole, with 24.4 percent of the school population receiving free or reduced lunch and 5.5 percent of students receiving English language learner services. The school consists of a primarily White student body, with small percentages of varying ethnicities also represented.

The opportunity to participate in the art club was made available to all 5th-grade students, and the timing of the meetings was constructed to be more accessible to free and reduced lunch students, many of whom attend aftercare at the school already. Students could choose to sign up for the club through the completion of a short essay expressing their interest and upon obtaining signed parental permission. The essay portion of the application was included to gauge student interest, motivation, and commitment prior to joining the club in order to ascertain whether students would commit to attending and participating fully in the experience. All students who applied were accepted. Two additional students originally elected to join the club, with one boy representing a minority group. After missing several meetings, both students dropped out of the club, citing their reasons as forgetting to attend or choosing other activities to engage in during meeting times instead.

I began by reflecting on the lack of student voice I had previously seen demonstrated within elementary school settings. Indeed, the limited number of participants and their generally homogenous demographic makeup itself are data to suggest limitations on student voice. It seems only some students are willing to participate in extracurricular activities of this nature. There is validation for the exploration of enhancing student voice, for even in the primary years, children have demonstrated the ability to develop leadership and communication skills on issues that directly affect them (Lundy, 2007). One must wonder, then, why opportunities to develop these skills are not generally provided until the intermediate or secondary stages of education.

## Art Club Meetings

In the art club I intended to develop student voice by first creating a safe and trusting environment among all participants. The initial meeting consisted of the students working together as a whole group to develop a name for their club, followed by an activity where they each created a personal sketchbook to record ideas and responses throughout the program (Table 5.1). During that meeting, participants completed a presurvey to assess competencies in leadership and communication skills. After developing a sense of community, I facilitated an exploration of art appreciation and advocacy examples by means of a digital presentation. With this guidance, students worked together in subsequent meetings to design a community event that that would promote the arts, dividing into various groups and partnerships along the way to meet this goal. Although students began by focusing on one task, they began to rotate throughout groups as more opportunities arose for self-directed activities, such as the preparation of decor and development of event communications. These activities included new forms of art production I introduced, including printmaking (Figure 5.1) and poster development (Figure 5.2).

## Hosting Art Fest

Chosen as the culminating event for the art club, Art Fest granted students the opportunity to conceptualize, plan, host, and lead an event for their community that consisted of four different art-making stations designed to promote the arts, including quilt square design, face painting, kindness rocks,

**Table 5.1. Overview of Activities in Art Club Meetings**

| Meeting | Activities |
|---|---|
| 1 | Foster a sense of community through development of club name (Young and Creative Art Club); sketchbook production |
| 2 | Examine why the arts are important and look at examples of student advocates; brainstorm and develop a cohesive goal of implementing a community Art Fest event |
| 3 | Whole group discussion—students develop plan for how to reach objectives (logistics of event—needs/resources/stations to host) |
| 4 | Whole group planning for event—division of responsibilities (Communications, Decorations, Advertising) |
| 5 | Implementation of student ideas and plans related to individual and group responsibilities |
| 6 | Continued implementation of student ideas |
| 7 | Continued implementation of student ideas |
| 8 | Preparation for event—identifying needs |
| 9 | Participants host Art Fest—community art-making event |

**Figure 5.1. Poster developed during student-directed collaborative activity**

and a collaborative mural (Figure 5.2). Each station was led by at least two participants, and the students developed a rotation schedule for themselves so that everyone had the chance to engage in each area (Figure 5.3). Additionally, students hosted a refreshment stand and acted as greeters at the entrance to the event.

Enhancing Elementary Student Voice Through Art and Advocacy        91

**Figure 5.2. Kindness rocks**

**Figure 5.3. Students' concept for the rotation schedule**

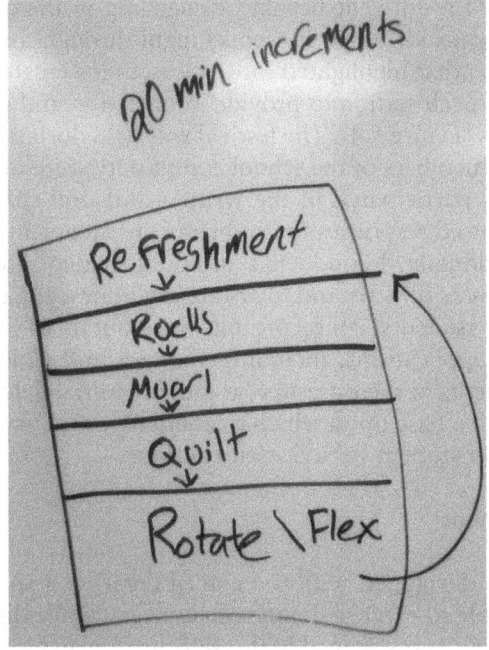

**Figure 5.4. Informational station advocacy signs**

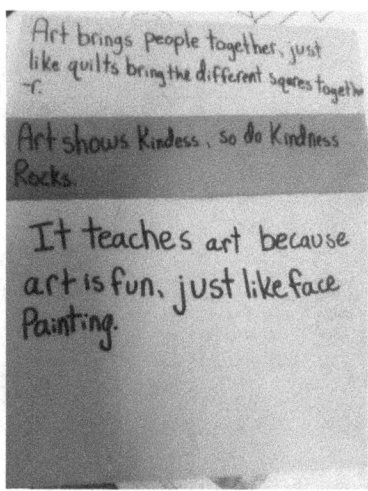

Most supplies for the event were borrowed from the art supply closet. Due to school district fundraising and donation restrictions, I provided the rocks. Participants reached out to the administration and the school's food service provider to obtain donations of refreshments for the festival. Centers were conceptualized by students with the purpose of promoting the arts. Each station represented a different benefit of engaging in the arts. During prior meetings, participants identified concepts taught through the arts and worked to develop stations that highlighted those ideas. Signs created by participants were displayed at each station to provide information and establish meaning with event visitors (Figure 5.4). The festival was held during the evening in the cafeteria, and all members of the school community were invited to attend.

Each student participated in the written and oral surveys voluntarily, and I coded and used responses to establish consistency in the development of themes. Additionally, I conducted audio and video interviews to gauge participant responses directly and to ensure my honest engagement with and representation of students. All recordings were obtained through the use of my cell phone's applications, including Camera and Voice Recorder. The responses of students in their presurveys and my initial field notes of student behavior provided a base upon which to compare post-survey responses and final reflections on student behavior and actions.

### Teacher Involvement

The art club was developed with the aim of creating a space in which students would be able to explore themes of advocacy while directing their own learning. Before students engaged in this self-directed exploration, I prepared them by developing activities that encouraged relationships among and with participants. The first meeting began with students working together to formulate a name for the group. Student involvement was encouraged through the arrangement of students in a circle. I guided students to share their ideas for a club name and taught the basics of effective communication with students. These fundamentals included turn-taking when speaking, hand raising, and active listening practices. During this activity, many students were hesitant to share ideas and only responded with my prompting.

Following selection of the club name "Young and Creative," the students created sketchbooks in which to record their ideas. Participants had their choice of materials with which to design their covers. Participant Shelli was one of the last students to select her materials, choosing to work with the same paint as a large group of her peers. The group produced their own designs, but Shelli and others asked me to procure materials and demonstrate processes frequently.

I introduced concepts of youth voice and advocacy as a guiding theme for the club. As the meetings progressed, I encouraged students to set a common goal for the club to host an Art Fest for the school and the surrounding community. Students set objectives for the event and determined individual responsibilities for helping the whole group achieve these objectives. These responsibilities included creating decorations, promoting the event, and obtaining needed permission and items for the festival, among others.

After participants had determined their individual responsibilities, they began to engage with the materials and processes of their choosing. I consistently encouraged experimentation and frequently reminded the students that they were in charge of the project. On one occasion Shelli saw flowers made from coffee filters outside of the club setting and wanted to attempt the process herself. She demonstrated increased autonomous behavior by choosing to create these decorations for the event and independently selecting materials to use. I directed her to the location of available materials but allowed her to experiment with production on her own. Shelli experienced failure in her initial attempt but independently identified and utilized correct materials during the following session. With her mistakes, she took the initiative to utilize the first-draft flowers as circles in a welcome sign (Figure 5.5).

This example contrasts with Shelli's behavior during the first meeting, in which she and her peers continuously sought teacher guidance and instruction in order to produce their sketchbooks. In this case, the minimization of teacher involvement facilitated the production of student work that served as a voice to welcome visitors to the Art Fest. This shows that, in lieu of the common practice of adult leadership, elementary students demonstrate the ability to grow independently and share their ideas. Owen appreciated his independence from teacher-guided tasks, saying, "My least favorite part of the Art Fest was the first few parts where we didn't really get to (make our art) . . . we did like a lot of (surveys) for you but not like real art and stuff" (interview, 11/09/18).

**Figure 5.5. Shelli's sign welcoming visitors**

**Autonomy and Risk-Taking**

Since an aspect of the study was to promote opportunities for student voice to be expressed, I gave participants many opportunities to make decisions and determine the direction of their experiences. When children make decisions and direct their learning, they connect with their ideas and can determine the messages they wish to share (Kohn, 1993). By limiting teacher involvement to that of a facilitator, students had the opportunity to problem solve and took charge in developing an event promoting the arts. Student interview data showed that the club provided a unique opportunity for students to work autonomously, with participants stating their favorite part about the club was that they got to organize the Art Fest on their own. Owen stated, "[The part of club I enjoyed most was] that I was able to organize an event to show why art is important" (interview, 11/09/18). Adeline showed appreciation for the new opportunities the club provided, saying, "You can exercise your creativity and you don't get to do that much in school. Because it's mostly do this, do this, do this" (interview, 11/09/18). Merry agreed, sharing, "I got to plan an event. I had not done anything like that before" (interview, 11/09/18).

Student use of time and materials demonstrated an increased amount of autonomy as the meetings progressed. During the first meeting when creating sketchbooks, they worked together with large groups that consisted of their previous acquaintances and utilized the same materials. One student, Charlotte, sat by herself and was hesitant to explore the materials available. During the penultimate session, students showed growth in independence, breaking off into smaller groups or working in isolation based on their individual goals or materials needed.

An example of an activity in which students were able to exercise their voice was during the production of advertising for the event. They had the choice to create posters that invited community members to attend or that shared messages with the community. Participants chose the materials they would like to utilize and the designs of their posters. Many students chose to communicate a message within their event poster, sharing ideas that they identified as important.

The increase in opportunities for student-directed exploration facilitated participants' engagement in various risk-taking experiences. The utilization of one's voice requires a level of courage—understanding that one's ideas and opinions will be heard opens one up to vulnerability. Therefore, chances to take risks with materials and experiences have the potential to overcome any hesitancy that may arise in the future to use one's voice.

Participants displayed the highest growth in willingness to take risks in the area of material use. One student wanted to create paper flowers but found that white glue would not hold the petals together. She researched alternative ways of producing the flowers and found that a hot glue gun might be effective. The student told me that she had never used a hot glue gun and was apprehensive about it. I demonstrated safe and effective methods for using the glue gun and encouraged the participant to try to use the tool. During the following meeting, the student attempted to use the glue gun. She burned herself at first and was nervous, but persevered and ended up utilizing it correctly to complete her task. After meeting her goal, she then demonstrated how to use the glue gun to other students to help them reach their goals as well. During an interview, the student recognized her achievement, stating she showed leadership qualities by demonstrating the new technique to others. By engaging in activities that required risk-taking behavior, the participant was able to share experiences and knowledge with others.

## Communication and Leadership Skills

That I regularly offered student-directed art-making opportunities ensured frequent chances for peer interactions. These interactions were key in developing the communication and leadership skills needed to enhance student voice. During the initial meetings, participants faced difficulties in communicating with one another to share ideas. Several students shouted their ideas, and many students talked over one another. With my facilitation of active listening practices, students learned to work together to plan and achieve common goals. In later sessions, participants demonstrated better communication skills, taking turns to speak and raising their hands to share ideas. Owen shared that he felt his ideas were heard during the club because "we all worked together so even if I didn't propose an idea, I agreed with other people's ideas and I supported them" (interview, 11/09/18).

Upon engaging in the art club, participants initially responded that using their voices meant they would have the opportunity to talk. Survey results after the club ended showed that students' views on voice had changed. Participants shared that having a voice now meant they would have a say in things and be able to share and put their ideas into action. This finding indicates that students learned to place importance on the quality of their voices and the impact they could have.

Charlotte especially showed growth in her ability to effectively communicate her thoughts and opinions. During the initial meeting, Charlotte responded that she didn't feel that her opinions were heard unless she were to speak up. After attending the art club, Charlotte stated she felt her opinions were heard. She also shared after the club that being a leader meant that one has to "take charge, and it doesn't always have to be vocally like a team captain or something. You know they are searching to be an example for others" (interview, 11/09/18). Charlotte was witnessed engaging more with others as well. During the initial meetings, Charlotte chose to sit by herself and was hesitant to share thoughts and ideas unless prompted by me. She did not demonstrate any attachments or relationships with fellow participants. During the final meeting and the evening of Art Fest, however, Charlotte displayed higher levels of engagement with peers, rotating through stations to help others and helping to problem solve rotation schedules. Additionally, Charlotte took charge of various art-making stations during the festival, explaining processes and advocating for the arts to visitors. When the time came to end the night and go home, Charlotte shared how important the club had become to her, stating her desire for all the participants to come back together and expressing her sad emotions that the club was ending (personal communication, 11/06/18).

Students demonstrated a shift in their views of themselves as a leader, with 100% of participants stating that they saw themselves as a leader at the conclusion of the investigation. In contrast, only 71% of participants identified themselves as a leader at the beginning of the study. Although the number of participants and percentage difference is small, surveys did suggest that students certainly value leadership, and seem to have worked toward developing it.

## CONCLUSIONS

This study explored student-driven arts advocacy in an elementary after-school art club with 5th-grade participants. Students worked as a group to organize and host a night of art making at the school for the community. Participants ran art-making stations designed to promote visual arts. I found that student voice grew in relation to leadership and communication skills, with increased student autonomy and a willingness to take risks developing in the process.

Although there are several examples of students developing voice and autonomy at the intermediate level (Bryant & Daniels, 2008; Buffington, 2014), there is little to be found on arts advocacy by elementary students and its potential to enhance student voice. My research endeavored to address this deficiency by detailing how elementary students were provided the opportunity to engage in advocacy through the arts and utilize their voice as a result.

Several challenges arose during the course of the study. With the young age of participants and their inexperience with group advocacy opportunities, students did not come into the study prepared to communicate effectively with one another. Significant amounts of time were devoted to developing basic communication skills of the participants, including the practices of active listening and voice control. A limited time frame and a lack of funds meant several student ideas for events and activities, including an auction to raise money, were not possible.

Although participants were unable to realize some of their initial fundraising ideas, they were able to engage in several opportunities that were previously unavailable. These included an art club and Art Fest, which served as a new connection between the students and their community. A large turnout to the event was noted, and participants shared that community members expressed appreciation for the students' accomplishments in organizing and hosting the event (Personal Communication 11/06/18).

I began this study with the hope that students would find an outlet for their voices through the arts. By placing value on the thoughts, opinions, and ideas of these youth, students were able to advocate not only for the arts but for themselves as well. Participants demonstrated their innate value as contributing community members and validated their right to do so in the process. Future studies could explore the potential for student leadership at an increasingly younger level, working to identify at what point students are able to begin developing their voices and leadership skills. Students developed personal connections during the experience and expressed growth in their relationships with others, with one student stating, "[The thing that I enjoyed most was] being with other people and actually thinking that I'm part of something" (interview, 11/06/18). By developing these connections as well as their voices, students gained experience in leadership and communication to carry with them in the future.

## REFERENCES

Bryant, J., & Daniels, S. (2008). Power, voice, and empowerment: Classroom committees in a middle level language arts curriculum. *Voices from the Middle*, 16(1), 31–41.

Buffington, M. L. (2014). Power play: Rethinking roles in the art classroom. *Art Education*, 67(4), 6–12.

Felleman-Fattal, L. R. (2017). Action research in preservice teachers arts-integration pedagogies for social justice teaching and learning. *Childhood Education, 93*(1), 66–72.

Kohn, A. (1993). Choices for children: Why and how to let students decide. *Phi Delta Kappan, 75*(1), 8–16,18–21.

Lundy, L. (2007). "Voice" is not enough: Conceptualising Article 12 of the United Nations Convention on the Rights of the Child. *British Educational Research Journal, 33*(6), 927–942.

Prettyman, S. S., & Gargarella, E. (2013). The power of art to develop artists and activists. *International Journal of Education & the Arts, 14*(2.7), 1–14.

Serriere, S. C., Mitra, D., & Reed, K. (2011). Student voice in the elementary years: Fostering youth-adult partnerships in elementary service-learning. *Theory & Research in Social Education, 39*(4), 541–575.

Soundy, C. S. (2012). Searching for deeper meaning in children's drawings. *Childhood Education, 88*(1), 45–51.

*United States: Is Obama's win also a victory for children's rights?* (2008, November 5). Retrieved October 10, 2018, from http://www.crin.org/en/library/news-archive/united-states-obamas-win-also-victory-childrens-rights

CHAPTER 6

# Self-Efficacy
Empowering Young Artists

*Jodi Fenton*

People's beliefs about their abilities have a profound effect on those abilities.

—Albert Bandura

Working for many years with K–5 elementary students, I have witnessed time and again students' frustration, excuses, and unwillingness to put forth effort in schoolwork. I have seen an avoidance of failure many times in the art classroom, which may initially be perceived as defiance. It often begins with an exasperated student declaring "I can't do this!" or "I suck at art!" Researchers found that individuals' efficacy expectations for themselves drive behavior and the belief of an expected outcome (Bandura, 1977; Flynn & Chow, 2014). Therefore, it is reasonable to believe that a strong sense of self-efficacy would lead students to perform a task with effort and positivity, because they would expect that they will have a successful outcome. In contrast, a lowered sense of self-efficacy may prevent students from attempting to perform a task, as they expect themselves to fail. This lowered sense of self-efficacy can lead to self-handicapping (Berglas & Jones, 1978).

Many students have a low sense of self-efficacy, especially when it comes to art making. Using reflective journaling, I wanted students to experience and understand that creating art requires effort and practice, much like learning a musical instrument or playing a sport. Students often allow themselves to make mistakes and persevere in these endeavors, but they seem to expect themselves to "naturally" be good or bad at art making. I wanted to find out whether the act of reflective journaling could be a way to empower young artists and dispel this notion of a fixed rather than growth mindset. I wanted to discover more effective and individualized ways to raise self-efficacy in my young students. How can reflective tools build self-efficacy? And what tools are better than others? How does utilizing traditional pencil and paper, digital recording, or peer discussion compare in effectiveness for students' reflections?

## SELF-HANDICAPPING AND PERSEVERANCE

In the article "Drawing on Curiosity," Ron Wigglesworth (2017) discusses the "I can't draw" cognitive gap. This happens when "children develop a resistance to progress in drawing when schematic representations are achieved, and the majority do not go on to develop graphic schemas or syntax in perceptual drawings" (p. 292). In other words, when drawing gets more difficult and requires more skill and attention to detail, children often give up before developing the skills they need to improve.

Self-handicapping is defined as "any action or choice of performance setting that enhances the opportunity to externalize [or excuse] failure and to internalize [reasonably accept credit for] success," (Török et al., 2018, p. 1176). Avoiding responsibility and self-preservation are two aspects of self-handicapping that relate to my research with elementary art students. Another aspect of self-handicapping is self-preservation. As described by Török et al., "Self-handicappers strive to protect and/or enhance their positive self-image and others' positive views of them by blurring the connection between their abilities and performance" (p. 1177). The use of this self-preservation technique is to safeguard one's feelings of self-worth. These perceptions of self begin in childhood and are carried into adulthood (Török et al., 2018). Some students who are capable—i.e., have no known emotional, behavioral, or learning disabilities—but are afraid to try and fail or risk being teased by peers, are kept from attempting the process. These students will self-preserve to avoid feelings of shame and failure at all costs. Stating that they "can't" do the assignment or they "suck" at the activity allows them to protect themselves against that feeling.

There is a strong connection between what we think and how we behave. Many of the behavioral challenges that educators must help students overcome are not examples of children acting out; instead, these derive from a lack of self-efficacy. People have a strong need for self-preservation. In avoiding responsibility by preemptively deciding that one could fail, behaviors may emerge. Having taught in public school for 19 years, I have worked through many behavioral situations with students. Helping students raise their sense of self-efficacy has been one of the most challenging. This is where a strong impact can be made in the K–5 art classroom.

Perseverance is the ability to follow through on a task, and it plays a role in self-efficacy. Perseverance and grit are key words in the philosophy of Schools for Rigor, which is the model for the district in which I teach. The term "rigor," as referred to in an educational setting, describes the learning experiences and educational expectations that are academically, intellectually, and personally challenging. For students to perform with rigor, they must display perseverance and grit.

Relating to the Schools for Rigor model, to have a class perform rigorously, they must display "courage and resolve in the persistence of doing something difficult," which is the definition of perseverant grit (Usher et al., 2019). Perseverance is when someone is willing to work at something despite how difficult it may be or the lack of immediate gratification it may provide, while grit is showing courage and resolve. To display perseverant grit, students must have a high sense of self-efficacy. For example, a classroom modeling Schools for Rigor will have students

- Working "harder" than the teacher
- Asking difficult questions and pushing on their learning
- Highly engaged due to the cognitive complexity of performance task and group work
- Questioning each other with higher order questions and high autonomy

These tasks, among others, require a high sense of self-efficacy (cognition) and a willingness to persevere (behavior) for students to achieve successful performance.

Teaching students to be perseverant is important, but I questioned how to teach perseverance to students who think they will fail before they even try. Usher et al. (2019) found a connection between perseverant grit and self-efficacy. In examining competing mediation models that showed self-efficacy as being a requirement for perseverant grit, it is not necessarily a prerequisite for self-efficacy. This finding implies that the focus must be placed on self-efficacy. A study from the same article reaffirmed my suspicions about the relationship between self-efficacy and perseverance. Through work with more than 2,400 public elementary and middle school students, researchers showed that one central facet of "grit" did not directly predict achievement in reading and math; however, self-efficacy did. "Only those with higher self-efficacy were rated as more competent. Popular school interventions that aim to increase students' grit without also increasing students' beliefs in their own academic capabilities will not likely ensure students' success in core academic subjects" (p. 878). Self-efficacy is focused on what one thinks one can do, the feelings of whether one is able to accomplish something or not. Concomitant with perseverance is providing students mastery experiences and verbal persuasion.

Mastery experiences, also referred to as mastery orientation, happen when someone is successful in a completed task and they can therefore expect to be successful again when completing the same task. These tasks, however, must be relatively rigorous so that the person feels a sense of accomplishment. This can occur in the elementary art classroom when practice and routines are put in place with scaffolding, which many teachers employ. For example, when students know that they will be using a medium that has been practiced in previous classes, they are less intimidated to use that medium in a more formal project. Mastery experiences are considered the strongest of the influences of self-efficacy.

The second influence, verbal persuasion, consists of receiving encouragement from a respected or trusted person (Kelleher, 2016). Praise must be authentic, specific, and about effort and perseverance. It is very important for the teacher to have built a relationship with a student for that student to respect and trust the praise and/or encouragement to persevere.

## FOSTERING STUDENTS' SELF-EFFICACY THROUGH REFLECTIVE JOURNALING

During 4 weeks in 2020, I conducted an action research project with two art classes of 5th-grade students to study how reflective tools build self-efficacy. Reflective journaling can serve as self-therapy, as a personal collection of thoughts and ideas, and can contribute to students feeling that their actions and behaviors have an impact on their own lives. Reflective journaling provides students the means to become self-aware and explore in a low-stakes setting. I used different tools to foster self-reflection in the art room: traditional journaling, digital journaling with Flipgrid, and partnered reflection. Journaling may take on a variety of forms and serve multiple purposes, benefiting students both academically and emotionally. I wanted to see if there was a connection between journaling and self-efficacy; whether with prompts, journaling could guide students away from self-handicapping strategies.

The two sections of 5th-grade art students that I studied included a total of 35 students, 18 from Mrs. A's class (11 girls and 7 boys) and 17 from Mrs. B's class (9 girls and 8 boys). Within Mrs. A's class, 3 students had Individualized Education Plans (IEPs) for special education services, and 3 had 504 plans for accommodations. Two students with IEPs were also English language learners (ELLs). Of the students from Mrs. B's class, 5 had IEPs for special education services, and 1 had a 504 plan for accommodations; there were no ELLs.

During the month of October 2020, there were 2 weeks of 100% virtual learning due to COVID-19. The school district transitioned to a hybrid model of learning on October 19, in which students attended school in person for half of the week, either in a Monday–Tuesday cohort or a Thursday–Friday cohort. Four of the 35 5th-grade students included in my research continued in the 100% virtual learning option. Due to COVID-19, much of my instruction and students' reflecting and creating used more technology than what would normally be employed in person at school. There was a huge learning curve for students as well as teachers. This format of learning virtually influenced the quality of student work as well as the percentage of work that was submitted. Students created their artwork with whatever materials they had available to them at home. In most circumstances, this was very limiting for students. Not being present in person,

I could not provide materials for students beyond what our school provided: Sketchbooks, pencils, pencil sharpeners, crayons, colored pencils, and markers had been given to any students who did not have them. The school district provided laptops to each student and hotspots as needed. Even when students returned to school in person part time, students were not allowed to share any materials at school. This was again very restrictive. In many ways, the challenges of COVID-19 make the study on self-efficacy even more illuminating.

I used three different types of reflective tools with students: sketchbooks with prompts (traditional), Flipgrid recorded self-reflections with prompts (digital), and partner reflecting. Each student experienced each of the three types of reflective tools during two art-making projects and answered questions about the tools in a survey at the conclusion of the research project. The lessons on which they were asked to reflect included planning and creating an abstract artwork based on the work of artist Alma Woodsey Thomas and planning and creating a self-portrait.

I began with a survey about prior successful and unsuccessful art making that students have experienced through their elementary years. I was pleased to see that most students who answered the question "How confident are you in art class?" felt either confident or extremely confident in their abilities. It is important to note that I substituted "confident" for the term "efficacy" to alleviate any discrepancies due to students' misunderstanding of terminology. About one third of students felt "somewhat confident," while none of the 5th-graders reported feeling "not so confident" or "not at all confident." Being aware that students may be hesitant to label themselves as confident or not confident, I included a follow-up question asking students to disclose with whom they felt comfortable sharing and talking about their artwork, presuming that the more confident someone feels about their artmaking skills, the more likely they are to want to share it with others. More than half of my students felt comfortable sharing their artwork with classmates or anyone who wanted to see it. About one third were only comfortable sharing their work with the teacher or a partner. Only one student said they were not comfortable sharing their work with anyone. The answers given provided credibility to the previous question about self-confidence.

During our first lesson, creating an abstract work of art inspired by the artwork of Alma Woodsey Thomas, students used the traditional style of reflection by answering questions about their process and artwork in their sketchbooks. Students were learning 100% virtually at this time, submitting all work and reflections by photographing their work and submitting through Canvas.

For the second lesson, creating a self-portrait, I taught students how to use Flipgrid to record their reflections on their planning and process. Partner discussion also took place during this lesson. At the time of this lesson, students were attending in-person classes for half of the week. On the days of in-person classes, students were socially distanced in the art classroom. They were situated at the ends of 6-foot tables, which still allowed for interactive reflection through partner discussion.

A final survey was administered at the end of the 4-week learning and research period. This survey included questions regarding preferences in artwork style and if and how the reflection process affected student's self-confidence (self-efficacy). When answering the question "Which artwork did you enjoy more?" there was a nearly even split between the abstract artwork and the self-portrait. More important, I also asked students why they preferred one project over the other. Identifying why students prefer one style over another can be a reflection on their sense of self-efficacy based on previous and current master experiences. Students tended to prefer what they think they can do well. Confident or extremely confident artists were more likely than somewhat confident artists to enjoy creating artwork that made them think or allowed them to be creative. Summer responded, "I liked doing the self-portraits because I had to think." Xander commented, "I liked the abstract art most because it was more creative." All students who viewed themselves as somewhat confident in the beginning survey gave reasons of "easy" or "fun" to answer why they enjoyed a particular project. Student answers appeared varied based on their sense of self-efficacy in creating their artwork.

From the survey, I expected to find that there would be a strong preference for one type of reflecting. I found, however, a nearly equal divide among the three types of reflection processes. This is significant because it shows that students need a variety of options to reflect. If students are to increase their sense of self-efficacy in art making through the reflecting process, they must be able to choose the method of reflection with which they are most comfortable.

When asked "Did reflecting have a positive effect on your confidence in your ability to create artwork?" student responses were, again, almost even. A little less than half of my students replied that reflecting did not affect their self-confidence. I wanted to know if students answered the way they did because they were already confident or extremely confident artists. I expected that students may not view reflecting as having an impact on their self-efficacy if they already saw themselves as confident artists. I found that only one third of students who reported being already confident or extremely confident in their art abilities responded that reflecting had a positive effect on their self-confidence, while two thirds said it did not. Of the students stating that they were somewhat confident, half stated that one of the three reflection processes had a positive effect on their self-confidence, including the one student who was not comfortable sharing her artwork with anyone.

While the literature and studies I reviewed spoke highly of using journaling as a mode of increasing self-efficacy, I found my own research pointing to students needing choice in the type of reflections in which they could participate. All the literature I found focused on the traditional style of journaling to reflect. I found that only one third of my students enjoyed this type of reflecting and fewer than that felt it helped their self-confidence. To influence self-efficacy, students need the opportunity to make choices not only in the tools and genres in which they create, but also in the ways they are allowed to reflect.

## CONCLUSIONS

In my study I focused on finding out if reflective writing would influence student self-efficacy. Second, I sought to shed some light on understanding if the tools used to reflect made a difference in the influence on student self-efficacy. Finally, I wanted to discuss what it means to decide not to participate, because I had some students choose not to participate in the study.

Did reflective journaling really affect students' sense of self-efficacy? My findings suggest that students often viewed reflections as "more work" rather than part of the artistic process. In general, student answers were short and shallow. More thoughtful answers were given by a few students who considered themselves to already be confident artists; however, it is difficult to tell if their answers reflected their self-confidence or their artistic/academic vocabulary without having an actual conversation with them about their answers. Typically, I would dig deeper with my students, but being online due to pandemic restrictions did not allow the opportunity for one-on-one discussions.

Was the method of reflection consequential? Again, the findings showed a nearly equal divide between students who preferred reflecting with traditional pencil and paper, digital platform, and peer discussions. Most students participated in all three types of reflection. However, there were many more missing reflections than I had hoped for. This may have been due to the inconvenience of the pandemic and not being able to show and discuss with me in class. It may have also been because I assigned specific types of reflections. If I had taught and students practiced all three types of reflections at the start of the year, they could have chosen which type they wanted to complete each time. Perhaps there would have been a better completion rate of reflections had that choice been in place, as well as a higher sense of reflections positively affecting students' self-efficacy. Having such an even split in preference of reflecting told me that students want choices. I witnessed this again when seeing such an even split of favor for projects and again when I asked students which media they enjoyed working with most. I also found that giving students choices for how to turn in an assignment led to a higher rate of work completion.

What does declining to participate in this research project say? That, too, is voice. But should it be considered an example of low sense of self-efficacy, or the influence of outside factors? As with considering why people may not exercise their right to vote, there are myriad possibilities. Some consider it a waste of time and eschew the system. Others are prevented due to external factors. Others may not know how to vote and avoid trying something they've never learned how to do. In this study, perhaps the students used avoidance, a self-handicapping technique, by choosing on the first day not to have their work included. The highest rate of incomplete work was from the six students who replied "no" when asked if I could include their artwork and responses in my research paper. In fact, of the six students, they each turned in 5 assignments of the 12 assignments given. Only one self-reflection was turned in by one of these six students. The reflections were included within the 12 assignments. Was this due to self-handicapping or the pandemic? Through nearly two decades of working with elementary age students, I have witnessed self-handicapping, coined by Berglas and Jones (1978), which is used in the absence of a strong sense of self-efficacy through avoiding responsibility and self-preservation. The pandemic provided another barrier for my students struggling with low self-efficacy.

Where do we go from here? I recommend that any teachers wanting to increase the level of self-efficacy in their students must provide them with options. Having choices in how to create as well as how to reflect can certainly benefit young artists. Despite the mixed responses I received in my research, asking students to reflect on their work as well as their successes and failures is still a worthwhile activity. Students need to try different ways of reflecting and make their own decisions on what works best for them; this allows for reaching as many students as possible. If they are to gain any value from what they do, they must be given some autonomy to choose what works best for them. Had I built in more reflecting opportunities for my 5th-graders in art classes in previous years, they may have had greater success with it the year of my study. I intend to deliberately build practices into my curriculum that offer multiple methods for reflecting. I also plan to introduce reflection to much younger students than I have in the past so that they can become comfortable with the process and use it as a master experience to increase their positive sense of self-efficacy.

## REFERENCES

Bandura, A. (1977). Self-efficacy: Toward a unifying theory of behavioral change. *Psychological Review, 84*(2), 191–215.

Berglas, S., & Jones, E. E. (1978). Drug choice as a self-handicapping strategy in response to noncontingent success. *Journal of Personality and Social Psychology, 36*(4), 405–417. https://doi.org/10.1037/0022-3514.36.4.405

Flynn, D., & Chow, P. (2014). Self-efficacy, self-worth and stress. Retrieved from https://www.thefreelibrary.com/Self-efficacy%2c+self-worth+and+stress.-a0506951828

Kelleher, J. (2016). You're OK, I'm OK. *Phi Delta Kappan, 97*(8), 70–73.

Török, L., Szabó, Z., & Tóth, L. (2018). A critical review of the literature on academic self-handicapping: Theory, manifestations, prevention and measurement. *Social Psychology of Education, 21*(1), 1175–1202. https://doi.org/10.1007/s11218-018-9460-z

Usher, E., Li, C., Butz, A., & Rojas, J. (2019). Perseverant grit and self-efficacy: Are both essential for children's academic success? *Journal of Educational Psychology, 111*(5), 877–902. http://dx.doi.org/10.1037/edu0000324

Wigglesworth, R. (2017). Drawing on curiosity: Between two worlds. *The International Journal of Art & Design Education, 36*(3), 292–302.

# Part III

# BUILDING COMMUNITIES THAT CARE

*Samantha Goss*

Students and their educational context are filled with layered networks and adjacent communities. Community informs democratic efforts and should also benefit from it. The following chapters reflect the complexity of community. Congdon (2004) identifies the three most common interpretations as "community as location or site, community as shared personal or group identification, and community as common purpose or set of beliefs" (p. 6). In previous chapters, the role of choice and voice in the art classroom empowered students to investigate and communicate their perspectives, needs, and goals. These resulting actions occur within communities. Dewey (1916) viewed community as where we are able to connect with others. Through shared activities and goals, we deepen our understanding of each other and invest in our community, making it possible to establish beneficial paths for future progress.

Approaches like community-based art education seek to locate art learning within the context of the local community as well as consider how learning can support change (Shields et al., 2020). A community context embraces the assets of the surrounding community while considering the effect we can have on our world (Bastos, 2012; Gude, 2009). Dewey (1916) urged that positive change is an outcome of a democratic society. Congdon (2004) echoed this, noting that communities are grounded in their beliefs and values, which can evolve through artistic practices over time. In the following chapters, students engaged in learning art by taking action for positive change in their communities and witnessing their impact. The case studies in these chapters are an example of an art education not solely focused on content or reinforcing existing social norms, but developing democratic citizens.

Chapter 7 demonstrates how choice and voice must also be taught in the context of community. Ashley Cardamone's service-learning art project required her students to first gain insight from a representative of the humane society in order to determine collective goals or shared interests for the project. Students were then able to make choices related to their individual work. By interacting with the humane society at the beginning and end of the project, the use of choice and voice occurs within the broader community. Cardamone's study is strongly rooted in Noddings's ethics of care supporting Dewey's desire for the habits of mind pertinent to democracy, such as an awareness of others. The dispositions of care and democratic life cannot be assumed and must be nurtured throughout a student's education (Dewey, 1916; Noddings, 1984/2013). At the end of the project and study, students expressed that they could see their ability to help the community and participate in the positive change that is so integral to a democratic society.

Community art provides a shared interest for a wide variety of citizens, including students. In Chapter 8, Lauren Roush details the creation of a community mural with elementary students from two schools during the pandemic due to her belief in community arts' ability to bring people together. Her goal was to help students see themselves as agents of change. From the beginning, students voiced their desired outcome for the mural, something that conveyed their positive and unique collective identity. Students actively chose how to represent diversity in their community with subjects ranging in race, ability, and age. Often they did not choose to represent themselves, but people from their community they observed in places like the park. The students noticed how their teacher incorporated all their ideas into the mural, fueling their ownership and investment in the work and community. At the end of the study, 11 out of 13 students felt more connected to their community. Roush demonstrates how even in elementary school, students can use their personal capabilities for a shared purpose that benefits their entire community, living Dewey's hope for education in a democratic society.

Those two chapters reflect a common occurrence in art education: helping students explore their connection to and role in their broader community. In contrast, Chapter 9 focuses on the school community in particular, and welcomes adjacent community members, like families, to participate. A new school building provided many welcome upgrades but sacrificed some of the visual remnants of the prior generations of the school community. Michelle Cox hoped a collaborative mosaic would help create a sense of community in the new building, which displayed more commercial and local professional artwork than student work. She welcomed family members into the school community where they participated in mosaic workshops. This allowed them to progress from feeling adjacent to the school community to more solidly connected. Families and students were excited to see their voices and efforts in the mosaic and looked forward to the long-term impact and expanded sense of school community.

Dr. Wendy Miller is adept at building community among undergraduate preservice teachers, and maintaining that sense of solidarity as students become practitioners. She seamlessly weaves her research, her teaching, and her service together by taking preservice teachers to work with alumni, and together facilitating projects that reach into the community at large. She thereby practices what she preaches, modeling in the real world a mutually beneficial system of connections that supports students, educators, and the communities in which they live, study, and work.

## REFERENCES

Bastos, F. (2012). Artful cityscapes: Transforming urban education with art. In K. Hutzel, F. M. C. Bastos, & K. J. Cosier (Eds.), *Transforming city schools through art: Approaches to meaningful K–12 learning* (pp. 13–23). Teachers College Press.

Congdon, K. (2004). *Community art in action*. Davis.

Dewey, J. (1916). *Democracy and education: A introduction to the philosophy of education*. The Free Press.

Gude, O. (2009). The 2009 Lowenfeld Lecture: Art education for democratic life. *Studies in Art Education, 62*(6), 6–11.

Noddings, N. (2013). *Caring: A relational approach to ethics and moral education*. University of California Press. (Original work published 1984)

Shields, S. S., Fendler, R., & Henn, D. (2020). A vision of civically engaged art education: Teens as arts-based researchers. *Studies in Art Education, 61*(2), 123–141.

CHAPTER 7

# Art to the Rescue
## Exploring Arts-Based Service Learning

*Ashley M. Cardamone*

Serving communities is a valuable experience for students during their K–12 school careers. Traditionally, many local school districts have required students in specific elementary and secondary grade levels to log a number of community service hours as part of their educational experience. This study explores a more structured, reflective, and reciprocal practice—service learning. In art education, it is common practice to encourage imagination and creativity within each lesson. Implementation of service learning in the art classroom offers the potential for students to transform their imagining into investigating, creating, and ultimately caring for their community. Service-learning experiences can help students develop care so that they are motivated to take action and impact their communities in positive ways.

There are many factors that contribute to one's development of sensitivity and empathy toward others, or what Nel Noddings (2002) refers to as an "ethic of care." Noddings points to the societal value of responsibility and moral strength. She says,

> Caring parents and teachers provide the conditions in which it is possible and attractive for children to respond as carers to others. We show them how to care. Children educated in this way gradually build an ethical ideal, a dependable caring self. A society composed of people capable of caring . . . will move toward social policies consonant with an ethic of care. (p. 223)

In my study, I facilitated a service-learning project with a group of 9th-grade students. The project focused on animal welfare, which was geographically pertinent, as the midwestern state in which I teach is home to the second-highest number of "worst" puppy mills, according to a report released by the Humane Society of the United States (2016). By working through a service-learning project relating to animals, the caring that students do for others can be increased. This learned and conscious caring enriches students' "ethical domain," and the empathy they develop has the potential to transfer to human relations (Noddings, 2013, p. 149). I partnered with the local humane society to include students in the various aspects of a service-learning project. Through this partnership, students were able to have authentic experiences that informed their planning, goal setting, art making, and reflection. Such personal work through service learning with a local partner is one way to increase relevance and encourage students' care and empathy for others.

Many art educators have facilitated research projects that center on indirect forms of service learning, such as Empty Bowls (Buffington, 2007). While this type of project connects to art curriculum and has the outcome of providing service to those in need, it often excludes many critical components of service learning, which I included in my study—student involvement in planning and goal setting, collaboration with the community partner, reflection, and reciprocity.

In this chapter I will review my study, following a foundational discussion of the ethics of care. Then, I will describe the development and implementation of my service-learning project. Finally, an analysis of participants' experiences and outcomes will be shared. The following research questions drove the study:

- How can arts-based service learning help students to develop empathy for others?
- How can arts-based service learning encourage students to become active citizens in their community?
- What methods and strategies are effective for teaching arts-based service-learning projects?

## ETHICS OF CARE

Nel Noddings (2002), a main proponent of ethics of care, discusses the importance of teachers educating children in a manner that encourages them to develop their caring selves. She writes that the adoption of care ethics by children can ultimately lead to a more caring society that advances policies consistent with its values. Noddings (1984) defines caring as interpreting experiences from the perspective of another and considering the needs and expectations of another rather than those of oneself. She goes on to describe building an ethic of care between those that are the "ones-caring" and those that are the "cared-for." Care ethics, much like service learning, require reciprocity. Noddings (2013) explains the value of animals' role in care ethics.

> We must ask then about the possibility of reciprocity in our relations with animals. It seems obvious that animals cannot be the ones-caring in relation to human beings but, perhaps, they can in some sense be genuine cared-fors. Is the form of their responsiveness . . . to require our adoption of an ethical attitude toward them? (p. 149)

In order to better equip students to respond to their diverse realities, it is important that they are explicitly taught how to adopt an ethic of care. As Noddings (2002) has described, children need adults—specifically parents and teachers—to model caring behavior in order to develop their own ethics. Children need opportunities "to respond as carers to others" (p. 223). This study offers an example of an arts-based service-learning project in which the "cared-fors" are animals. Service learning has a wide range of benefits to all parties involved. Among the most significant is an increase in student empathy for others (Bowdon et al., 2015). This type of growth corresponds with students' role as the "ones-caring" in service-learning projects. My study aims to demonstrate the ways in which service learning in the art classroom can increase student empathy and foster an ethic of care.

Service learning is an approach to teaching that combines the following components: strategic planning, community service, reciprocity, connections to academic standards, and reflection (Buffington, 2007). Successful service-learning projects rely on an extended relationship between a school and the community organization to be served. This relationship is based on working in a reciprocal manner in which both parties benefit, as opposed to students simply volunteering to benefit a particular group or log a required number of service hours (Montgomery et al., 2015).

Wade (2001) describes service learning as a practice in which students may take action to work toward social justice. Through service-learning projects, students can take action in different ways. "Service-learning projects might involve direct service to individuals in need, indirect service such as fundraisers and collections, advocacy activities . . . and research and community education." (p. 26) Regardless of the approach to service learning, Wade also notes the importance of mindset as students complete projects. It is important for students to consider themselves not as noble do-gooders, but as important members of the community who share the responsibility to make it a better place, and benefit when conditions improve. This is caring-for, rather than simply caring *about*.

The project implemented in my study takes an arts-based approach to service learning. In this case, students take action through art making. Krensky and Steffen (2008) write that in this approach, the arts are involved in both the teaching and learning components of the project. They also identify key criteria that differentiate arts-based service learning from service learning in other content areas. There must be a focus on "arts-based educational objectives ranging from creative self-expression to competency with discipline-specific standards" (p. 15). Students must be learning arts content, as well as using the arts to meet the identified community need, and will ultimately become connected to their community through their artistic voices. The opportunity for artistic expression within service learning can empower students and motivate them to work toward a specific goal.

## OVERVIEW AND PREPARATION

My qualitative research explored the experience of junior high art students who participated in a service-learning project related to animal welfare. These students were enrolled in a 9th-grade art class that met for 46 minutes every day. Of the 21 participants in the project, 6 were boys and 15 were girls; 2 identified as African American, 1 as Asian, and the rest as White. The school reported 584 enrolled students with 22.2 percent participating in free and reduced lunch programs in fall 2016.

Through my project, student participants learned about local shelter animals and their living conditions, created paintings, digitally turned the paintings into greeting cards, and sold them to raise funds for the local humane society. At key points during the project, students had direct contact with the humane society. They also completed written reflections that provided more insight into their learning and experience.

### Guided Activities and Discussions

Students spent approximately five class periods working through guided project preparation activities. I began our first class by asking students a question, "What is a portrait?" Students told me everything they knew about portraits, and many students' first response was to blurt out something about how portraits are of people or faces. As students continued to discuss and dig deeper into what portraits might include, I kept a list of their responses on the board. They continued to get more descriptive and give examples of some famous portraits they knew. When I asked students what the purpose of a portrait was, they became more thoughtful and decided that portraits can show personality, tell a story, and come in many different styles. I told the students that we would be creating portraits, but with animals as our subjects. After that, we looked over our list again. I asked students which of the things they knew about portraits were still true if the portrait was of an animal. We circled each item that applied.

Over the rest of that class period and the next, students completed an activity called "Dogs" from Lynda Barry's *What It Is* (2008). The activity encouraged students to recall animals from their memories, consider animals' perspectives by writing stories, and begin to deal with animals visually. Following the activity, the project became more local. Students spent some time exploring the local humane society's website. Each student selected three shelter animals (either cats or dogs) that stood out to them and wrote in their sketchbooks about why they chose each one. Students' reasons for choosing animals varied from how they looked to the way their personalities were described on the website, or the animal's similarity to animals they had known.

The next class period was spent discussing what the format of the actual art project would be. Students voted on the media for the project and, as a group, selected painting. I also introduced students to the idea of service learning as something that connects learning in school to impacting communities, and works toward a specific goal (Buffington, 2007). Their next step was to brainstorm questions and potential goals for their project, as a visit from a humane society representative and shelter animal was scheduled for the next day. Using the humane society's website, students explored needs within the facility and made lists of questions in preparation for the visitor.

The following day, a representative of the local humane society came to visit and brought with her a shelter dog who was up for adoption. During the visit, she shared with the students that the facility is completely donation-run; she also provided data about intake, adoptions, medical services, and costs associated with caring for animals at the shelter. As the representative spoke, she walked around the classroom so the dog could interact with the students. She also led students through a discussion comparing the life of an animal waiting to be adopted at the humane society with the life of an animal living in a permanent home. She asked students about their own pets and what they thought their pets were doing right now. Answers included eating, sleeping, or sitting on the couch looking out the window. She then described what life is like for a shelter animal waiting to be adopted: the space they live in, noise and comfort levels, the number of strangers they see a day, etc. After her presentation, the volunteer answered students' questions and discussed the potential fundraising goals they had brainstormed the previous day. The visit concluded with time for students to practice sketching the representative's dog from life.

**Goal Setting**

When implementing service-learning projects, a critical step is goal setting, which is also an essential skill within our state's core standards. I wanted my students to set their own goal for their project, so I facilitated some activities that would help them decide what effect they believed was most important for them to have on the shelter animals. I began the next class period with a discussion about the visit from the humane society representative. The discussion led into an image theatre activity in which students used their bodies to create silent sculptures (Boal, 2000). Students divided themselves into two groups. One group illustrated the life of a shelter animal; they arranged themselves to communicate with students acting as various animals in the same enclosure with people looking in, knocking, and taking pictures (Figure 7.1). The other group illustrated the life of a pet living in a permanent home by arranging themselves to show a pet laying on a couch, under a roof, and being petted by its owner (Figure 7.2).

**Figure 7.1. Image theatre portraying animals in a shelter**

**Figure 7.2. Image theatre portraying a pet in its adopted home**

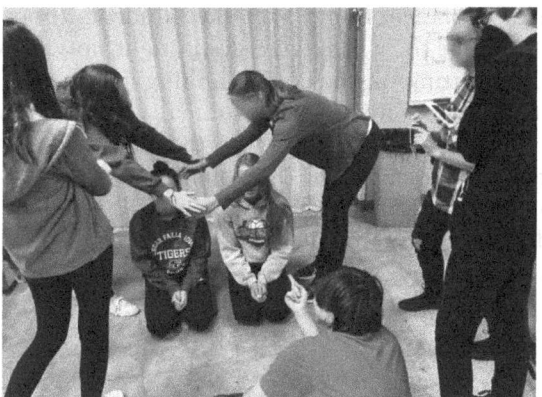

Following the activity, students completed a written reflection on what they learned from the humane society representative's visit, and we began to discuss project goals more realistically. Our humane society visitor had helped students to narrow all the potential goals they had generated into three that were most relevant to the shelter: (1) new toys for the animals, (2) contributions to medical costs, and (3) food for dogs at the shelter. Students used this information to make these goals more specific and timely. Each individual student chose the goal they most wanted to work toward and wrote this preference at the bottom of the reflection. From there, they shifted their focus to creating of their artwork by revisiting the shelter animals they had selected and written about in their sketchbooks. They each chose one animal, then began sketching it on large paper as the first step for creating paintings.

I reviewed students' goal preferences for the project and discovered that most of them wanted to contribute to medical costs. The humane society representative had shared with us that total medical costs at the shelter were approximately $3,000 per month. I discussed this goal with students, and we all agreed that it was unrealistic with the price point of the items they would be selling and the time frame in which they needed to be sold. Students decided instead of raising funds to cover all medical costs for a month, they wanted to focus on the funds needed to spay and neuter all cats for a month. I contacted the shelter and learned that the average monthly cost is $1,030. I shared this with students, and they agreed that it was a reasonable goal they wanted to meet.

## ANALYSIS OF THE ANIMAL PORTRAIT PROJECT

Students spent the next several class periods working on their animal portrait paintings. The requirements of the project were that they needed to use some kind of paint to create their portrait, and that it needed to be inspired by an animal from the local humane society. During these classes, I offered a variety of painting demonstrations and artist examples, as well as one-on-one guidance for students.

Once students' paintings were complete, we installed them in the school's art display case and included a write-up of our inspiration for the project, including that there would be more to come soon (Figure 7.3). Over the next couple of weeks, students' paintings were digitized, turned into greeting cards, and printed. Following that process, students spent a class period folding cards, packaging them, and labeling them for sale (Figure 7.4). They began selling packs of cards that day to friends at school, family, neighbors,

**Figure 7.3. Display wall**

**Figure 7.4. Cards packaged for sale**

and other members of the local community, and continued for approximately 3 weeks. I collected the funds raised and kept a running total for students, then turned money into the school's bookkeeper.

Before the semester ended, I decided the students' donation would be best delivered to the humane society in person through a class field trip. I scheduled a trip, and set up a selling deadline for students. Ultimately, students raised $900 for the local humane society by selling 150 packs of four cards at $6 each. They were $130 short of meeting their goal, but were excited to deliver their donation.

Nineteen of the twenty-one students who participated in the project were able to attend the field trip. The class spent approximately one hour at the humane society and participated in a tour, presented their donation (along with any leftover cards for the humane society to continue to sell), and interacted with the shelter animals. At the culmination of the project, students completed additional written reflections. The most revealing written reflection came at the end of the service-learning project when students responded to the following questions:

1. What did you like most about this project?
2. What would you like to be different about this project if we were to do it again?
3. How did it make you feel to use artwork to improve the community?
4. How might you use art to take action in the future?
5. What is the most important thing you learned during this project?

The main focus of my research was to explore the experience of junior high art students who participated in a service-learning project related to animal welfare. I hoped to discover effective methods for teaching arts-based service learning, as well as the ways in which service learning promotes ethics of care and motivates students to take action in their communities—to see themselves as *part of* a community of care.

The research data I gathered were student-produced materials including written and drawn project preparation activities, artwork samples, and written reflections from key points throughout the project. I also recorded field notes of my own observations and collected photographs of teacher-guided class discussions that were outlined on a classroom whiteboard. In data analysis, the theme of helping emerged. It became clear that creating artwork in order to help others had a variety of effects on students, and that those effects had reciprocal relationships with helping. This type of reciprocity is a key element of service learning (Noddings, 2013, p. 149), and the data I collected in this study support the significance of the relationships between what students give and what they receive through service-learning projects. Three main themes emerged: teaching strategies, art skill development, and achieving the purpose of the service-learning project. Connecting all three was the theme "helping." The idea of helping others came up in many ways across the data and often was connected to one of the other themes.

**Teaching Strategies**

In this project, students were offered a great deal of choice in the way they created artwork. This allowed them to have a personal voice, which made the work more meaningful. When students were asked what they liked most about the service-learning project, 15 out of the 21 student responses indicated that they liked having choice within the project. Some students most enjoyed having the freedom to choose the shelter animal that would be the subject of their paintings. A few students wrote they liked that they got to "choose any animal" they wanted to paint. One student wrote, "I liked that I got to choose my animal and how I painted it." Her response showed the ownership she felt over the subject of her work, and also pointed to what many other students appreciated—choice of artistic style.

Students expressed the importance of having freedom to work in whatever style of painting they wanted. Some students described it simply, by saying they got to "make [the painting] the way you want." Others described making a choice about style as "making it your own," "having freedom," or "having individuality and not being forced to do anything." One student explained that she liked painting more on this project than in the past because she "got to paint stuff without worrying about it being realistic."

The variety within the body of student artwork created during this project illustrates the level of freedom and choice students had in regards to both subject and style. Students were introduced to many different painting

**Figure 7.5. Student examples**

techniques through demonstration and visual examples. Student work samples, including those in Figure 7.5, show the diverse ways in which students chose to use the art skills they developed throughout the project.

The student voice that developed in the artwork because of freedom with subject and style contributed to the level of engagement students had in the project. Student engagement in the project, as a result of teaching strategies, transferred to engagement in the task of helping others. I observed and documented in field notes that there were many class periods during which all students were engaged, particularly during the painting portion of the project.

It was clear that the engagement had grown from staying on task to helping the shelter animals. Each work day, students at three or more out of the six tables in the classroom had conversations with one another about their shelter animals. On multiple occasions, students shared why they had chosen the shelter animal that was the subject of their paintings. One student entered the classroom with a great deal of energy because she had just found out the subject of her painting had been adopted. She celebrated and shared the humane society's Facebook post about the adoption with the rest of the class. Another student came in before school one day during the project to tell me that she and her mother planned to adopt the cat that was the subject of her painting. These examples show the significant impact this project had on students. Giving them the choice of their subject and how to approach the subject in their work encouraged them to care more about helping the shelter animals their artwork would ultimately benefit.

## Art Skill Development

Another significant thematic category that emerged from the data was the value students placed on art skill development. It was important for students to build skills as they created their artwork so they would feel confident not only selling the work, but also putting it out into the community for others to see.

Some students appeared more concerned with building skills during this particular project, compared to their previous work in the course, since the work would be used to help the shelter animals. This presented itself in a variety of ways. Two students who typically worked faster than the rest of the class slowed their pace considerably as they painted their animal portraits. The reason for this change was that they were both more conscious of "mistakes" in their artwork than they had been in the past. I worked with each of these students individually to help them to work through what they felt were mistakes in their artwork. When asked what he liked most about the project, one of these students wrote, "The way that if I messed up, I went with it and added changes." When the same student was asked what he would like to be different about the project if he were to do it again, he wrote, "I would not change anything because it looks better than I originally planned." His completed painting shows many of the "changes" he added to his project after one-on-one instruction about art techniques: adding a border, filling space, outlining to create cleaner edges. His artwork shows significant growth throughout the span of the project (Figure 7.6).

**Figure 7.6. Student artwork progression**

Other quotes taken from student reflections also demonstrate their appreciation of art skill building during the project. Student responses included that the skills they learned were "new to me because I've never painted a dog before," and "pretty cool because I understand how to use paints better." Another student wrote that what he liked most about the project was "the fact that we were helping our community and learning art at the same time." Sixteen other students echoed this sentiment in their written reflections. The purpose of building skills in this project was to help others, and data show that students made that connection. Helping students to build their painting skills gave them the confidence they needed to create successful artworks, and to raise funds for a worthy cause. The community connection also gave a tangible relevance to the learning that happens in art class.

**Achieving the Purpose**

Although the students did not achieve their monetary goal, they used their artwork to earn a generous donation they were proud to deliver to the local humane society. When asked how it made them feel to use artwork to improve the community, 19 out of 21 students responded positively, with the other 2 students responding in a neutral manner. Some students specifically referenced their motivation to build skills. One student wrote, "It made me feel good about my artwork. I had never really been confident with my artistic ability and knowing that it was being used to help the community really helped that." Other students referenced the achievement of a goal as what made them feel good. A student responded, "It made me feel really positive to benefit the community through my schoolwork as it showed these projects can actually be useful." He continued to describe that working toward the donation goal was "the best aspect of this project." Helping others encouraged motivation in the students, and their motivation enabled them to create quality work for the purpose of helping.

With many service-learning projects, a goal is for students to develop a greater sense of empathy and care. Many components of the project implemented in this study strengthened students' sense of empathy and care. The greatest theme that emerged from the data, helping, can be interpreted as caring. Some form of the word "helping" was used 61 times across all the student-produced data that I collected. This is an effect of the construction of the project and the scaffolding created by project preparation, the classroom visit, and the field trip to the humane society to enable students to reach a point of caring about the shelter animals they worked to help.

Although facilitating this service-learning project took much longer than a traditional art project, the additional time spent on project preparation, goal setting, and reflection contributed to the growth students showed in terms of empathy and care, specifically for shelter animals. The empathy and care students develop for animals transfer directly to their sense of empathy and care for other humans. Noddings (2013) explores this idea and writes, "many of us experience in our encounters with animals' feelings very like those we are familiar with in genuinely ethical situations" (p. 148). In this way, participating in this particular arts-based service-learning project pushed students to develop their own ethics of care and self-efficacy, and will hopefully encourage them to take action in their communities in the future. Indeed, students stated that from this project, they learned that they could "change the outcome for someone else," and "use artwork to improve the community." One student stated, "It was incredible to make a school project into something that will benefit more than just us. The most important thing I learned was that helping the community can be fun and beautiful."

Arts-based service learning, particularly at the junior high level, has the potential to build students' confidence and help them to further discover their own identities. Reflections contained many heartwarming phrases, such as "warm and fuzzy," that are rare to hear from 9th-grade students. A student even confessed, "Well . . . helping the community in any way was, to me, an entirely foreign feeling. I'm usually pretty selfish, but this made me feel good about myself." Despite the challenges that arose during this study, and the time investment required by service-learning projects, the benefits are of immeasurable value, and show students that they can create positive change in the world throughout their lives.

One particular student involved in this study was so invested in her work that she wrote an article in the school newspaper about the project. It was titled, "Art to the Rescue." In this study, art came to the rescue of animals in need. Witnessing my students creatively take action gives me hope that they will continue to come to the rescue of those in need throughout their lives, and that their caring will make the world a better place. Personally, I have benefited from maintaining partnerships with community organizations through annual service-learning units in my art classroom. These units now include learning not only about the local humane society, but also local wildlife rehabilitation and the local nature reserve. In broadening the community groups with whom I work, I have also learned about the media that best suits service-learning projects. While I initially had students create paintings, printmaking allows us to raise the most funds because we can hand-print cards instead of making a painting and paying for the printing. I have used service learning beyond the curriculum in the classroom as well. Whenever the school has a "fun day" in which students choose activities, I offer a service option with one of our established community partners. For example, for our most recent school "Hoopla" event before winter break, we collected donations for the humane society in advance. When the society's volunteers came to offer their Hoopla session, they brought dogs to visit, and shared about the organization's work. In the session, students crafted blankets for the shelter animals to deliver to the volunteers along with the fundraised donations. From a small project begun 6 years ago, service now has become a part of our school's culture.

## REFERENCES

Barry, L. (2008). *What it is*. Drawn & Quarterly.
Boal, A. (2000). *Theatre of the oppressed*. Pluto Press.
Bowdon, M., Pigg, S., & Mansfield, L. P. (2015). Feminine and feminist ethics and service-learning site selection: The role of empathy. *Feminist Teacher, 24*, 57–82.
Buffington, M. (2007). The big idea service learning and art education. *Art Education, 60*(6), 40–45.
Krensky, B., & Steffen, S. L. (2008). Arts-based service learning: A state of the field. *Art Education, 61*(4), 13–18.
Montgomery, S. E., Miller, W., Foss, P., Tallakson, D., & Howard, M. (2015). Banners for books: "Mighty-hearted" kindergartners take action through arts-based service learning. *Early Childhood Education Journal, 45*, 1–14. https://doi.org/10.1007/s10643-015-0765-7
Noddings, N. (1984). *Caring: A feminine approach to ethics and moral education*. University of California Press.
Noddings, N. (2002). *Starting at home: Caring and social policy*. University of California Press.
Noddings, N. (2013). *Caring: A relational approach to ethics and moral education*. University of California Press.
The Humane Society of the United States. (2016). *The Horrible Hundred 2016: Puppy Mills exposed*. Retrieved from https://www.humanesociety.org/sites/default/files/docs/2016-horrible-hundred.pdf
Wade, R. (2001). Social action in the social studies: From the ideal to the real. *Theory into Practice, 40*(1), 23–28.

# CHAPTER 8

# Cultivating Connection Through Community Art

*Lauren Roush*

Humans need to be creative and feel connected in order to thrive, and community art is a way to meet the primal needs of humans as they create something new, form social bonds, play, and nurture care of and connection to others. It is also a way to envision what society can be and hold a mirror to what it is. Disconnection and lack of creativity perpetuates isolation, discontentment, and is detrimental to the health of individuals and communities (Blatt-Gross, 2017; Dissanayake, 1988, 2000; Lowe, 2000, 2001; Putnam, 2000). As Brené Brown (2018) claims, "We may have a couple hundred friends on Facebook, plus a slew of colleagues, real-life friends, and neighbors, but we feel alone and unseen. Because we are hardwired for connection, disconnection always creates pain" (3:37:18). Significantly, Brown (2013) asserts that "unused creativity is not benign; it gets metastasized. It has to be cultivated." Community art meets this primal need of humans to create and connect with one another, and envision the society they want to live in.

As individuals are engaged with their community and valued for their participation and creative abilities, community art fosters democratic engagement (Dewey, 2009; Gude, 2009; Mattern, 1999). Participants of community art create and play with a diverse group of people while creating a public artwork. The process of working together for a common goal brings community members together and cultivates a value for different voices—creating a stronger and more inclusive community (Berglin, 2017; Lowe, 2000; Lawton, 2019). Lastly, as individuals who participate in community art aid in the enrichment of their community, this action perpetuates a deep level of care for both the community and its members (Blatt-Gross, 2017; Noddings, 2005).

This chapter examines community art—specifically the creation of a mural—and the role a teacher can play in cultivating its creation in a small town with the help of 3rd- and 4th-grade students, as well as parents and community members. Borrowing from Hillery's (1982) and Lowe's (2000) definition of community, I consider the finite geographical location of a small midwestern town and its occupants a community.

Because students were not allowed to be in close proximity due to COVID-19 restrictions, I elected for a movable mural that could be separated into 16 pieces and reassembled back together. Additionally, this method gave students the agency to determine where in the community they would place the mural. I planned this mural project at a time when we were still socially distancing due to the pandemic, so some students were remote learners, and all in-person students were participating in a hybrid model of teaching. The need for connection, care of self and others, and a remedy for isolation and disconnect was, therefore, even more important.

Community art can be a catalyst for connection, value, care, civic engagement, and creativity among community members, thereby mitigating some of the detrimental effects of isolation. Students who participate in community art and feel validated in their engagement are more connected to the community, socially connected to diverse groups, and perceive themselves as agents of change. Further, they are active guardians of their own well-being, as well as the well-being of their community as a whole, and connect to the members of their community at a deeper level. This research investigated how community art projects develop care and connection for participants and on how I, as an art teacher, can support students in developing the skills needed to democratically engage with their community.

## OUTCOMES OF COMING TOGETHER PURPOSEFULLY

In my case study there were eight student participants from each of two schools—sixteen students total. School A has some middle-class or working-class families, but the majority of the student population are eligible to receive free and reduced lunch. Six girls and two boys participated in the mural project. The students ranged in terms of socioeconomic status and family life. School B has mostly working-class and middle-class families, with a smaller population of students who are eligible to receive free and reduced lunch. Five girls and three boys participated (one sibling set). The students ranged in terms of socioeconomic status and family life, including single-family homes and foster care. The participant group consisted of 3rd- and 4th-grade students who had shown interest in participating in extra art activities, such as staying in during recess to explore individual artistic interests, or completing independent projects on the weekend. I facilitated the communication between the eight students from each school by providing a shared Google Doc and meeting with each group separately. The students had agency in determining the design and the location where the mural would reside. Some students met in person, and some students used Zoom to participate from home.

Once the students decided on a design, I supported them with creating the design digitally. After the digital design was accepted by the students,

**Figure 8.1. The completed mural on marine plywood panels, 4' x 8', acrylic paint and varnish**

I cut a piece of 4-foot-by-8-foot plywood into 16 pieces. I created a grid within the design and transferred the image onto the 16 sections of plywood. Each student was given a section to paint. Once they were complete, I compiled the artwork back together, and installed it at the agreed-upon location in the community (Figure 8.1). Along with the installed artwork, we included a plaque explaining the art and providing a hashtag. Community members were encouraged to take a picture with the artwork and post it on social media with the hashtag. By doing this, community members were able to engage with the art—and others within their community—in a safe and socially distanced way.

This mural project is not my first involvement with community art. When I was a child, I was asked to help with several different murals that were installed throughout the community of Newton. These experiences helped solidify my interest in art; my engagement with my community made me feel valued and perpetuated a deep care for the well-being of my community and its members. Since then, I have been able to work on more public art with students.

Community art ignited my passion for art as a child and continues to be a way I serve my community on both a macro and micro level. I believe in the benefits community art has to offer. Confirming the research of Gude (2009), Lowe (2000), and Lawton (2019), my community art experiences have allowed me to work with a diverse group of individuals, from varying backgrounds, cultures, and ages, and increased my understanding and care for the participants I worked with and the communities we painted. Because we had time to talk, learn, play, and create together, positive social interactions led to feelings of connection, care, and feeling valued.

In the analysis that follows, I describe how the process of making the mural affected students' engagement, care for community, valuing of diversity, and general well-being. This research revealed several themes also in the literature: Community art is fun and encourages democratic engagement, which provides an avenue for students to value diversity and care for their community.

**Having Fun With Community Art**

It is important that community art creation involves a fun, safe, and accepting atmosphere (Hoefferle, 2012; Lowe, 2001). Students must feel valued in their efforts, safe enough to have fun, and enjoy their experience. Although community art projects are an aesthetic experience, the process itself is just as important as the final project. Lowe (2001) claims community arts projects should have a "common mood most conducive to a positive community art experience [which is] comfortable and playful [. . .] a safe space for interaction" (p. 460). Students took the community art project seriously, but after a few times of meeting as a group, students started to loosen up. Many students would make jokes, laugh, and act silly while brainstorming ideas or working on the project.

At School A, after the third meeting, students wanted to start painting their panel in the art room because they were nervous about bringing it home. They all joked and laughed with each other as they worked—even though they were in different grades and different classes. They asked to listen to music and talk while they worked. They talked about their lives, homes, families, and interests. One student who loved to paint was glad to have the opportunity to do it more.

At School B, as my facilitation became less didactic, students contributed their thoughts, generated ideas, and communicated their feelings without much prompting. They started to joke around with one another after the second or third time of meeting. After one meeting, students planned to go to the park to play. The connection felt during the collaboration on the community art project helped strengthen connection among group members that extended past the project.

Although the in-person students had a fun and playful experience, it was not initially clear as to whether or not the remote students would have the same benefit. It was hard for them, using Zoom to participate, to hear all of the conversations. Because they were attending the meeting online, they engaged with their classmates very little. The joking, laughter, and play came mostly from the students who were in close physical proximity to each other. However, upon reflection after the completion of the mural, when asked what their favorite part of the creation of the community artwork was, one remote student responded, "it was fun and I'm glad my teacher chose me." Additionally, other responses from in-person students of the same question included: "I had fun," "I enjoyed working with everything on the project," "it was fun and challenging to do but enjoyed it very much," and "it was a new fun experience." Students seemed to genuinely enjoy the creation of the artwork and working together.

**Encouraging Democratic Engagement**

Community art is a catalyst for democratic engagement, as it provides participants with a way to connect with their community and feel like agents of change (Dewey, 1927; Hoefferle, 2012; Lawton, 2019; Lowe, 2000; Mattern, 1999). Community art can play a vital role in the development and participation on which a thriving democratic society relies. Indeed, Lowe (2000) argues that the United States relies heavily on building communities through art, claiming, "publicly and privately, the arts are being recognized as assets that promote healthy communities and are gaining support as resources for intervention and prevention efforts" (p. 358). Community art serves as a catalyst for democratic engagement and is extremely beneficial to both people and communities because it promotes care, connection, and value for diversity by working toward a common goal.

During the first meeting with School A students, they actively contributed ideas to discussion while considering what their town needs and what they could add to the community art in Newton. When asked about including anything about the derecho storm that had affected the community in August of 2020, students were adamant about absolutely not including the storm. Similarly, when School B was asked if they wanted to do something with the derecho storm, one student responded, "I think Iowa has more things than just the storm." I asked what they meant, hoping they would elaborate more, and they explained that they thought focusing on the storm was limiting because Iowa and Newton had more positive things to offer. My thought was that art could be used to heal the trauma and stress, but the students were worried about the representation of the town. It was important to students that we frame the community in a positive way.

After initially seeing the tentative design, School B wanted to include a Maytag sign on the Maytag building because "Maytag is important to Newton." When brainstorming options for grants, both schools were very innovative about their ideas to fund the project. All of them wanted to either personally supply paint and materials, or explain the idea to local businesses and ask for supplies or money for supplies. Students were very engaged with ways to find the resources to fund the project.

Students collaborated and connected with each other, which was the intent. However, collaborating with me as the teacher and their family members was an important part as well. When asked what their favorite part of the project was, one student responded, "doing it with Ms. Roush" and another responded "spending time with my teacher." This project extended past just students and teachers to include parents and other family members. From the beginning students had asked if their parents or various family members could help with the project, and some students stated that their favorite part was, "having my mom help me with it," or, "having my dad work on it with me." The connection this community artwork provided was multifaceted, as the project connected students to their classmates, their community members, and the adults or family members who supported them.

Another example of family participation is when one student from School B came to me in my classroom and said her 4-year-old sister spilled paint all over her section of the community artwork and she couldn't see the outline of the dog anymore. She asked if I could redraw it so she could paint it again. I told her to paint everything else, then when she was done, I would help her redraw the dog so she could paint it. She clarified several times that she wanted to paint it, she just needed support with redrawing the dog. I never heard back from the student, and did not think it was time sensitive, so I did not touch base with her before going to the other school—School A. While at School A, the secretary called and said a family from School B was coming to talk to me. I became very worried and wracked my brain over what I could have done to cause a parent to hunt me down at another school. When they arrived, they brought the panel to me and asked if I could redraw it, as it was Friday and the student wanted to work on it over the weekend. The family was very supportive and involved with the project.

Upon completion and installation, one mother told me the story of showing her son the artwork. After picking him up, she decided to surprise him by driving past the mural. She did not want to say anything; she wanted her son to discover it had been installed in the community. She said, as she was driving by, her son yelled, "That's my mural!" and continued to refer to it as "his artwork," further reiterating the feelings of ownership the students felt over the community artwork.

Students from School B, especially, were very concerned with diversity and inclusivity in the mural. They critically analyzed diversity that exists in their community and advocated for representation, which is good citizenship and shows awareness of all community members. The *Newton Daily News* asked to do a story about the community artwork (Figure 8.2). Students were really excited about this opportunity, and they all sent in quotes about the artwork in hopes of their being included in the paper. Since students opted to have the community artwork at the Newton Public Library, students were asked to go to the library board meeting and propose the idea. Through this community artwork, students had the opportunity to share their voice, values, and opinions.

Shortly after the students finished their individual panels and turned them in, the district moved to a fully remote teaching model due to the high incidence of COVID-19 cases in the county. Regardless of the change to remote teaching, 13 out of the 16 students responded to an online survey about their

**Figure 8.2.** Feature in the *Newton Daily News*

community artwork. Out of the 13 who responded, all said they wanted to participate in a community art project again. One student responded that they "enjoyed making something for the community." During the brainstorming sessions, students had been encouraged to develop social consciousness about their community, and upon creation of the artwork, were asked to participate in ways that are avenues for future social change and political participation (Dewey, 1927; Hoefferle, 2012; Lawton, 2019; Lowe, 2000; Mattern, 1999).

Another student said, "I think that was nice of you to put all of our ideas in." As students discussed ideas and voted on decisions, a student commented on the democratic nature of the community art project, stating, "You put all of our answers in one which made me have a warm feeling." The goal of this research was to give students ownership of the project and agency in determining key decisions. Allowing students to take on a leadership role in the decision-making process provided them with skills needed to democratically engage with their community in the future.

As we have seen, community art is a catalyst for connection and engagement, and can remedy feelings of isolation (Blatt-Gross, 2017; Lowe, 2001). It provides benefits that meet people's innate needs: the need for connection with others and the need to create (Blatt-Gross, 2017; Brown, 2013, 2018; Dissanayake, 1988, 2000; Lowe, 2001). There were various things that students enjoyed about participating in this community artwork; many participants just simply liked the process of creating something. Students enjoyed connecting with one another and taking creative liberties in their artwork. For example, one student said her favorite part was "getting to design two extra characters," and another student liked "creating the nature, like people and trees." One student mentioned "that on [mine] it had a lot of extra colors," and many simply responded that painting was their favorite part. Although some students said the process was challenging, they always affirmed that they enjoyed the process greatly.

**Valuing Diversity and Caring for Community**

Community artwork encourages participants to think of people and things beyond themselves and take responsibility for the work—thus promoting care and valuing diversity within the community (Blatt-Gross, 2017; Noddings, 2005). Eleven out of the thirteen students who responded to the survey said they felt more connected to their community after creating this artwork. Students showed care for their community by caring about how it was represented, and opted not to include the destruction caused by the derecho storm. Students also exhibited care for community members when they advocated for representation and inclusion of diversity within their artwork.

Although the research literature indicated that valuing diversity plays an important role in community art, I underestimated what a large role it would play in the creation of this community artwork (Berglin, 2017; Dewey, 1927; Gude, 2009; Hoefferle, 2012; Lowe, 2000; Mattern, 1999). During our initial brainstorming session, issues of representation and inclusion took the lead. Two of the 3rd-grade students from School A were in the same class the previous year. That year, when they were in 2nd grade, we analyzed the murals that already existed in the community. One girl in the class, who was invited to help with the community art project but was unable to join, said, "I think Newton should make a mural with people who look like me and [redacted], because there aren't any." The student was African American, and was referring to another student who was also African American.

Two other students who helped with the mural were in the class the prior year when we had the conversation about the lack of representation of people of color in the community's murals. Student A is White, and Student B is African American. When our group was analyzing the murals that the community already had, Student A said, "Hey [Student B], remember when we thought the guy on the right was black?" Student B responded, "Yeah, I've seen it in person. He's not." This segued the conversation to inclusivity in our artwork. The students said they think it will be important to include lots of different types of people.

**Figure 8.3. Lady with service dog**

School B students were much more vocal and adamant about inclusivity, and were also very specific. For example, after I showed the tentative design for the mural to the students for critique, several students said that "there needs to be more people and more skin colors," meaning that the variation in skin color was not broad enough. To be more inclusive, they also asked to add somebody with a disability. They insisted on the inclusion of the panel on the lower right showing a service dog with a person who is blind, as the school had recently received a service dog (Figure 8.3).

School B's guidance counselor had obtained a grant to receive a Golden Retriever trained to work with children with adverse childhood experiences, so it is no surprise that the students advocated for a service dog to be included.

Additionally, students at School B specifically asked to give a baby to the couple pictured in a panel on the lower left of the mural, as they said that there were not enough kids or children in the artwork (Figure 8.4). School A's participants analyzed the panel with the couple closely, as it was a student from School B who had completed it. Students from School A were discussing the individuals, and one girl said, "These guys are either cousins, brothers, or really close friends," while pointing to the two men with a baby. Another student responded, "Or they're a couple." The first student reflected on that comment for a little bit, then responded, "They are either cousins, brothers, friends, or a couple."

During the critique of the initial design, one student specifically asked that we include a Muslim woman with a hijab. She said, "We should put in a woman with a head wrap," to which I responded, "Like a head covering? A Muslim woman with a hijab?" and she responded, "Yeah!" After our meetings, this student often plays at the park next to the school while she waits to be picked up. I drive by this park when I leave school to go home.

**Figure 8.4. Picture of couple with baby**

When I drove home that day, I saw Muslim women with their children playing at the park. This student, who is not herself Muslim, had critically analyzed the diversity that exists in the community and advocated for inclusivity and representation of community members with whom she interacts (Figure 8.5).

**Figure 8.5. Student's inclusion of a woman wearing a hijab**

## CONCLUSIONS

Community art is—and must be—fun, and it encourages democratic engagement by creating opportunities for collaboration and connection. This mural also provided students with an opportunity to analyze the diversity that exists in Newton and represent it—thus promoting care for both the community and community members.

The mural asked students to think beyond themselves, be cognizant of the place in which they live, and be responsible for creating something for it—thus promoting care. I facilitated the project in such a way that students could become fully engaged with the project. Students reflected on the representation of community members, sought support from family members and myself, connected with various people, and cared about the outcome. The majority of participants in this research—11 out of the 13 who responded to the survey—claimed they felt more connected to their community after creating this artwork. Facilitating an open space for collaboration allowed students to connect on many different levels.

The value of diversity within a community art project took a central role during the creation of the mural. In School A, we revisited previous discussions between students about the lack of diversity in the murals that already existed in the community. School B students were adamant about including a diverse array of people in the artwork. These students were cognizant about including a service dog, a person with disabilities, children, adults, different races, and different religions, in order to more accurately represent the community members of Newton.

Above all else, it is important that participants in community art feel that their efforts are valued and they enjoy their experience. Parents, teachers, family members, and the students themselves continue to tell me how much pleasure they gained from participation in the creation of the community art project. Students throughout the creation reinforced that it was their artwork, they reiterated the ownership they had, and they continually showed up to important meetings because they felt like key players in the creation. For example, some students attended a board meeting for the public library via Zoom to participate in the decision of where the community artwork would go and explained how it was created.

Facilitating a safe, enjoyable space for students' voices and values to be heard allows students to reap the many benefits that community art provides. Brené Brown (2018) found in her research about shame that 80% of adults she interviewed had something happen at school that was so shaming it changed how they thought of themselves. Brown states, "What makes this even more haunting is that approximately half of those recollections were what I refer to as creativity scars. The research participants could point to a specific incident where they were told or shown that they weren't good writers, artists, musicians, dancers, or something creative." It is detrimental to the health of individuals if they are shamed for their creativity or excluded from care and connection. Conversely, it is imperative to the health of individuals that they are creative, their efforts are valued, they enjoy their experience, and they feel connected to each other and their community (Blatt-Gross, 2017; Brown, 2013, 2018; Dissanayake, 1988, 2000; Lowe, 2001). Community art can be a catalyst for this enjoyable, creative experience by providing participants with the opportunity to connect and collaborate with their community members.

## REFERENCES

Berglin, J. (2017). An interview with Olivia Gude about connecting school and community arts practice. *Arts Education Policy Review: Policy and Community Arts Education, 118*(1), 60–66.

Blatt-Gross, C. (2017). Creating community from the inside out: A concentric perspective on collective artmaking. *Arts Education Policy Review: Policy and Community Arts Education, 118*(1), 51–59.

Brown, B. (2013). *The power of vulnerability: Teachings of authenticity, connection, and courage.* Sounds True Publishing.

Brown, B. (2018). *Daring greatly: How the courage to be vulnerable transforms the way we live, love, parent, and lead.* Penguin Random House Audio.

Dewey, J. (2009). *Democracy and education: An introduction to the philosophy of education.* The Floating Press.

Dissanayake, E. (1988). *What is art for?* University of Washington Press.

Dissanayake, E. (2000). *Art and intimacy: How the arts began.* University of Washington Press.

Gude, O. (2009). Art education for democratic life. *Art Education, 62*(6), 6–11.

Hillery, G., Jr. (1982). *A research odyssey: Developing and testing a community theory.* Transaction Books.

Hoefferle, Mary M. (2012). Floats, friendship and fun: Exploring motivations for community art engagement. *International Journal of Education Through Art, 8*(3), 253–269.

Lawton, P. (2019). At the crossroads of intersecting ideologies: Community-based art education, community engagement, and social practice art. *Studies in Art Education: What Does Social Engagement Mean and What Should Art Education Do About It? 60*(3), 203–218.

Lowe, S. (2000). Creating community: Art for community development. *Journal of Contemporary Ethnography, 29*(3), 357–386.

Lowe, S. (2001). The art of community transformation. *Education and Urban Society, 33*(4), 457–471.

Mattern, M. (1999). John Dewey, art and public life. *The Journal of Politics, 61*(1), 54–75.

Noddings, N. (2005). *The challenge to care in schools: An alternative approach to education.* Teachers College Press.

Putnam, R. (2000). *Bowling alone: The collapse and revival of American community.* Simon and Schuster.

CHAPTER 9

# Collaborative Art Making Between 4th-Graders and Community Partners
Its Impact on School Culture

*Michelle Cox*

When I first moved to a college town in a midwestern state, I taught at a neighborhood school that was an established landmark in the community. Built in 1931, this school had served elementary students for 81 years. The classic architecture, the outdoor classrooms in the ravine, murals painted by local artist Emily Vermillion, and mosaic planters created by students were a few characteristics adding to the ambiance of this historical building. Years of experiences and traditions had shaped this school and made lasting impressions on those who visited the campus.

In 2009, this community was shocked to learn that this old building would be retired and teachers and students would relocate to a new facility. Incentives like air conditioning, larger classrooms, and a gymnasium separate from the cafeteria made this transition appealing; quickly, faculty looked forward to the new location. I also had the opportunity to help design the layout of the art room. Architects listened to my input, from the number of sinks to the size of drawers and placement for storage. This was the dream of an art teacher—to be able to design studio space for their students. But several years in, I wondered

- What has been added to welcome visitors?
- What adds to the environment of the school, and brings students, faculty, and families together?
- What are the impressions students, parents, and visitors feel walking through the halls?
- What visual components contribute to positive school culture?
- Does artwork in the display cases matter?
- Is students' work hung outside homerooms?
- What makes this school stand out?
- Aside from the school's structure, what other characteristics have contributed to this school's culture?

Seeking answers to these questions, I launched a study to document the effects of creating and installing a collaborative, permanent mural for the school. Would it connect the physical building to the culture being built inside and out? I also wanted to find out whether a collaborative art project would help show the importance of the art program and, in turn, build a stronger art program. At the time, there was low attendance at the school's fine arts night. There also was comparatively little student-generated art on permanent display throughout the school, compared to commercial art. I personally felt the need to advocate for the importance art and art making has on a student's education. I asked: *Does collaborative art making encourage students, parents, colleagues, and community members to identify the impact art has on a school's climate/culture? How does this look?* Through this collaborative mural project, students, parents, and teachers would come together to create art. I believed it had the potential to raise awareness about how art education can benefit a school as well as build relationships through art making.

Current research supports the idea that collaborative art rooms contribute to a strong sense of community among students (Loh, 2015). Similarly, studies have shown the significance classroom culture has not only on the school but also on students and their relationships with their peers (Cummings, 2012). Research has indicated when intergenerational activities are paired with the visual arts, participants discover similarities, supporting a stronger sense of community (Whiteland, 2013). Such studies support the benefits of collaborative art making, but very little research shows how parents, students, and teachers together influence a school's sense of community through art making. Most studies that examine school culture focus on pedagogy in the classroom. Yet anecdotally, it seems that stakeholders such as students, staff, and parents in a school community have an influence on their school's culture. We all want the best for students and school. I sought to document how making a mural builds relationships and forms a positive school culture that supports the arts. I wanted to "demonstrate[s] that the arts are as important to students' intellectual development as math and the sciences" (Eisner, 2005, p. 8). By experiencing community art firsthand and meeting professional artists, students—and their caregivers—had the opportunity to experience art outside classroom walls and make a better connection to their community, adding to a positive feeling towards the arts.

Interacting with students, parents, and teachers provided me with a better understanding of their views on art and how it influences our school. Through this project, I wanted to encourage "a feeling of unity from shared activities that reflect a sense of common purpose" through art making (Adejumo, 2000, p. 12). I found that students, their families, and staff learned that students were capable of creating art that contributed aesthetic value to this building. The project helped create a bond between students, staff, and families while diminishing their prior perceptions of art education as a frivolous activity.

As soon as the school community was aware of the mosaic project, there was support from teachers, parents, grandparents, our PTO, and a local bank. The people who wanted to be a part of this communal project sent a powerful message in and outside of the school. Community members were as interested in working together as they were in enjoying the final product. Support in the form of monetary donations, attendance to the workshop and the mosaic tour, and words of encouragement all made this a cooperative work of art. Each group that contributed to the project experienced a sense of community enrichment as a result.

Our school has an overwhelming amount of commercial art and local artists' work on display. Those pieces create a friendly atmosphere, but it is important for students' work to contribute to the school's culture. "Student artists become more engaged, invested and serious about their work when they know the final product will be displayed in public" (Prahl, 2018, p. 8). Creating an opportunity for collaborative student work to be permanently and publicly displayed demonstrates an investment in the children at this school and demonstrates value placed on what they have created.

Hutzel's (2007) study showed how a collaborative art project promoted positive change socially and aesthetically in a community. Similarly, Carolina Blatt-Gross's 2017 study suggests art is the foundation of a strong community. She examined trends in school violence and attributed them to a lack of community, which has become a social norm in contemporary society. Blatt-Gross suggested restoring a sense of belonging in our communities to reverse trends in school violence, bullying, and gun violence. Like Hutzel, Blatt-Gross saw the strength in community art to reshape a community. She saw collaborative art making as a means to restore the sense of belonging that has been lost in our culture.

Reshaping a community is a process built from the inside out. It begins with the fundamental human characteristics in the brain, before it can effectively influence the community. Blatt-Gross (2017) suggested community art "cultivates a sense of caring, group solidarity, and collective identity" (p. 56) among its participants.

This corresponds with the need to inculcate care in our school curriculum. Blatt-Gross refers to Nel Noddings's (2012) curriculum of care to support the need to re-establish our sense of community. Noddings adds that caring is an essential skill in order for a community to thrive. When we teach students to care about themselves, then they are able to care for others. When we teach them to care about others, then they can care about the world around them. Blatt-Gross (2017) states, in education "collective art making offers a vehicle through which joint endeavors can facilitate connections and commonalities" (p. 52).

Cooper and Sjostrom (2006) encourage collaborative works of art and state that "schools are the best settings for collaborative arts" (p. 8). Cooper notes the educational value of collaboration because it requires conversing, negotiating, listening to one another, and finding solutions to problems. The skills students exercise are the same skills adults encounter at work and home. Students learn the democratic process when making decisions on a collaborative project. Generating student voice on artistic framework, artistic theme, shape, size, color, display, and closing ceremony is democracy in action. For this research study, participants interacted with existing art, and I solicited their ideas and input throughout the process, making it a constructivist learning experience for all.

## LAUNCHING THE COLLABORATIVE MURAL PROJECT

In my midwestern public elementary school, 4th-grade students, family members, and teachers participated in this qualitative study of collaborative art making. Three classes of 22 students each, totaling 66 children, agreed to participate; 28 boys and 38 girls. According to the district's database, 30 students identify as White, 19 as African American, 15 as Asian, and 2 as Hispanic.

The project involved both class time and weekend workshops, to enhance participation opportunities. Each class had one 54-minute art class in which 66 4th-grade students participated in mosaic making. Weekend workshops included 25 student/caregiver pairs. Some students attended more than one weekend workshop. Thirty-three relatives to the students participated in after-school workshops. These participants included 15 mothers of students, 7 fathers, 1 aunt, and 10 younger siblings who are students at the school. Seven teachers directly participated in the art production, and fourteen showed support for the project through email or conversation.

Students were introduced to the project during art class. They and their caregivers also had an opportunity to hear my presentation about the mosaic project at our back-to-school night. In both situations, we talked about the existing artwork in our school and places where a new permanent work could be installed. A 3' x 4' whiteboard served as a visual for students to gain a better understanding of the size of the mosaic and view examples of mosaics from the Internet.

In class, students and I used a map of the school to guide initial surveys. We took a tour of the school so that students could record their observations. After the mapping exercise, students indicated their favorite existing work and their top choice for the location of the mosaic. Photographs documented students' top choices about where the final piece should be installed. Students voted on the top two choices for a final destination. To determine the content for the piece, students brainstormed ideas in sketchbooks, explored one another's ideas, planned a final concept, and continued to critique and reflect reasons for content. The final mosaic resulted from a combination of ideas from sketches and student discussion.

Meanwhile, I organized a weekend tour for families to view local, professional works of art at different sites. Unfortunately, there was a low turnout due to severe weather and a 5-day weekend for students. Plans to visit one site were canceled because the road to the facility was submerged in water, but despite that setback, five families and one homeroom teacher attended the mosaic tour.

Participants met at school and carpooled to a public recreational facility where Gary Drostle's *River of Life* mosaic is housed (Figure 9.1). Participants walked on Drostle's work, which is part of the foyer floor, and observed color, shape, and formulated ideas about the artist's work. Ironically, Drostle's piece was inspired by a flood in this community in 2009, and the day of the tour, the river was once again swollen from the recent rainfall.

The group continued to a local recreational park to look at mosaic sculptures and were able to talk to the artist-coordinator for this project (Figure 9.2). This installation includes a park bench and ten 4-foot freestanding mosaic sculptures created by local 4th-grade and high school student artists. Even though the weather did not cooperate, the students found inspiration by the work they saw. Students ran around the park with umbrellas and raincoats, identifying objects in the sculptures. This installation made a lasting impression on them because they were surprised to learn children their age made these mosaics. Later in class, one student described

**Figure 9.1. Gary Drostle's *River of Life* mosaic**

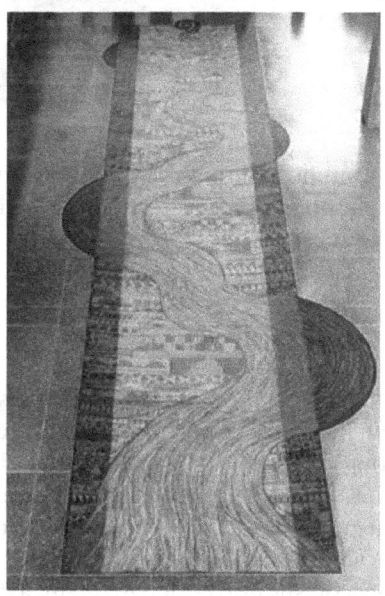

**Figure 9.2. Participants at park**

**Figure 9.3. Students observing mosaic bench**

her experience and communicated that the park bench was the most impressive work she saw on the tour. With self-doubt she asked, "We can't make something like that, can we?" (Figure 9.3).

## MAKING THE MOSAIC

From sketchbook drawings and group discussion, students decided the content of the mosaic democratically based on their own preparatory art (Figure 9.4). Through "student consensus, and democratic elections" (Cooper & Sjostrom, 2006, p. 20), the mosaic began to take shape. The school's mascot, "Norm the Bulldog," was significantly represented in a majority of student responses to surveys. From there, students sketched ideas of where the mascot should be located—in a field of wheat, outer

**Figure 9.4. Initial student sketches**

space, in a rocket, etc. This process continued until everyone agreed on the mascot standing in midwestern rolling hills, holding the world to represent the diversity of the school's student body, with nocturnal and diurnal animals represented under the day and night sky. The final draft came from student sketches and was determined to be a 4' x 5' mosaic.

A piece of white butcher paper in the same size was used for the original drawing made from student sketches. A duplicate was made in case the original drawing was damaged during production. A heavy piece of plastic was laid over the paper to protect the drawing from mosaic adhesive. Then fiberglass mesh was laid over the top of the plastic and covered the drawing. The original drawing was visible through the plastic and fiberglass mesh. Participants used mosaic adhesive to glue individual tiles to the mesh.

Using a template of the Earth, groups of four students experimented by fitting individual mosaic tiles onto the page to complete their mini mosaic. When each of the eight groups were finished, they had a gallery walk to see all the different versions of the "Earth" made by each of the groups. This activity helped familiarize students with the mosaic process before attending an after-school workshop with a guardian.

In the after-school workshops, students came back to school accompanied by an adult to participate in the mosaic making. Seven workshops were offered over a one-month period, and participants reserved sessions through Sign Up Genius. They were encouraged to stay for as long as they wanted and attend multiple sessions. When participants arrived, they reviewed a copy of the 4' x 5' drawing of the final draft and decided on a section to mosaic. While I set up the work area of drawing, plastic, and mosaic mesh, participants chose mosaic tiles for their color palette. They then laid mosaic tiles to their liking before gluing the pieces down. This process averaged 30 minutes for each group.

Of the seven after-school workshops scheduled, five were held, and two were canceled due to no sign-ups. In the first workshop, seven groups of students and guardians participated and in the last workshop two groups participated. Four weekend workshops had better turnout. They averaged seven groups per session. It was interesting to watch students and caregivers. Groups worked independently, and compared mosaic production to puzzle making, trying to find the perfect fit. Participants also described the activity as relaxing, and several commented on how fast the session went by. Younger siblings helped sort colored mosaic tiles, drew on paper, or played on an outdoor playground in direct view of the workshop. Occasionally participants would look at other groups' work and offer suggestions and compliments, but no two groups worked together on a section during any of the sessions.

## REFLECTING ON THE PROCESS

During the initial surveys when students were deciding the placement of the mosaic, they indicated areas of the school that are bare. Surveys indicated that 35 students felt the cafeteria was the top choice for placement. Other top choices were the west side stairwell and the main stairwell. During a class discussion, students were asked where the mosaic should be placed, and I had students give me a thumbs up or down indicating whether they agreed or disagreed. Someone suggested the stairwell, and several thumbs down were shown. When asked why, one student shared "not everyone will be able to see our work." He was talking about students who use wheelchairs. The majority of students were receptive to the needs of their peers, and based their decision on the placement of the final work to accommodate everyone in this school. Another student indicated that the cafeteria is a space in the school where all students go every day. These responses showed the participants' ability to empathize with classmates who might have had limited exposure to the final work due to accessibility.

In a post-workshop survey, Sheila indicated she enjoyed making the mosaic with her dad, but if she had the opportunity again, she would prefer making the mosaic with her classmates. Her explanation was that "everybody would be able to participate" (interview, 11/8/18). Sheila was aware that not all 4th-graders were able to attend after-school workshops, therefore eliminating some students' participation in the mosaic making. Sheila was attentive to the needs of others and had concern for those who could not attend workshops. From her response, mosaic workshops for each of the three homeroom classes took place during their scheduled art class.

During workshop sessions, several parents commented on the lasting impression the final artwork would make on the school. While working on the mosaic, a mother commented to her son how "this art will be hanging after you graduate from elementary school, middle school, and high school." (Figure 9.5) Another mother commented to her daughter how the work will be hanging in the school after she graduates "and will still be here when [her

**Figure 9.5. Mother and son working on the sky**

3-year-old sister] graduates, too." Students seemed unaware of the longevity of the mosaic until parents pointed out the permanence of the artwork.

In initial surveys, students commented on the need for color in the school. "All the walls are grey, so it [mosaic] will make it colorful. It's really plain in the cafeteria." In post-workshop surveys, several students commented on the legacy the project brought to the school when asked if participating in the mosaic was important. Emmett shared, "Yes because the mosaic will be in the school forever and it is nice to know that I was a part of it" (interview, 11/7/18). Similarly, Claire shared, "Yes because generations of Bulldogs will get to enjoy our work" (interview, 11/7/18). Students recognized their contributions to the mosaic as an asset to the school, and the legacy this project provided for future generations.

A conversation with a teacher echoed this same sentiment on lasting impressions, stating "this work will be something that will be in the school forever and now the students are leaving their mark" (personal communication, 11/3/18).

## CONCLUSIONS

The purpose of my study was to find a way to advocate for the arts at a midwestern elementary school through a collaborative art project involving 4th-grade students, parents, and teachers. My research showed the impact the arts have on this school's students and its broader community. Students demonstrated awareness of their peers when deciding the placement of the mosaic. They recognized this 4th-grade project extended to the student body and found a way to share their work with everyone who entered the building.

Parents, grandparents, aunts, former art teachers, local banks, professional artists, and establishments where mosaic art is displayed supported this study. The mosaic project served as a tool to open communication about the importance of the visual arts and provide a hands-on experience to make art. This project influenced this school and the 96 individuals who laid tiles one at a time. The complete work will serve as a reminder of the positive outcomes of collaborative work for years to come.

Besides monetary donations, the amount of support towards this project from colleagues and parents was overwhelming. Parents made comments during the mosaic tour and workshop sessions that they had interest in funding the project as needed. In addition, local artists extended their interest in supporting the project by talking to students about the mosaic process.

The project posed a challenge for some families who could not attend after-school workshops for various reasons. One student told me that she did not have transportation to school without the bus. An ELL told me she wanted to attend, but her mother did not know how to use Sign-Up Genius, therefore she felt she could not participate. Although I then provided a written schedule of workshop dates and times as an alternative, this family did not attend. During fall conferences, I spoke to a mother who said she would love to attend but worked in the evenings. When suggested that she come during the school day, she said that was when she was at her day job. Aware of these constraints, mosaic making was also done during class time.

On January 11, 2019, 4th-grade students, parents, and faculty viewed the final piece together for the first time. Participants watched a timeline presentation and saw how individual sections of the mosaic developed over a 3-month period. Students were thrilled to see the final work. They were eager to show their peers their contributions and share their experience (Figure 9.6).

**Figure 9.6. Students viewing the final installation for the first time**

## REFERENCES

Adejumo, C. O. (2000). Community-based art. *School Arts, 99*(6), 12–13.

Blatt-Gross, C. (2017). Creating community from the inside out: A concentric perspective on collective artmaking. *Arts Education Policy Review, 118*(1), 51–59.

Cooper, M., & Sjostrom, L. (2006). *Making art together. How collaborative artmaking can transform kids, classrooms, and communities.* Beacon Press.

Cummings, K. (2012). Classroom culture: Fostering relationships in the art classroom. In L. Campbell & S. Simmons (Eds.), *The heart of art education* (pp. 199–203). National Art Education Association.

Eisner, E. (2005). Opening a shuttered window: An introduction to special section of the arts & the intellect. *Phi Delta Kappan, 87*(1), 8–10.

Hutzel, K. (2007). Reconstructing a community, reclaiming a playground: A participatory action research study. *Studies in Art Education, 48*(3), 299–315.

Loh, V. (2015). The power of collaborative dialogue. *Art Education, 68*(5), 14–19.

Noddings, N. (2012). The language of care ethics. *Knowledge Quest, 40*(5), 52–56.

Prahl, D. (2018). Standing out for art. *School Arts, 117*(9), 8.

Whiteland, S. (2013). Picture pals: An intergenerational service-learning art project. *Art Education, 66*(6), 20–27.

CHAPTER 10

# Networks for Building and Supporting Art Education

*Wendy Miller*

Throughout the decade I spent teaching art in public schools, I took great joy in creating collaborative art projects with my students. We painted murals, created installations, and constructed large sculptures for our school. I often looked for opportunities to expand art making outside the four walls of my classroom. As I transitioned into teaching higher education, my energy for community art stayed with me, and it was contagious! Now, working with preservice and graduate students in art education, I have collaborated with hundreds of children, numerous community organizations, and dozens of art teachers throughout the state and internationally.

There is a natural reciprocity of learning that takes place in working with communities and in maintaining connections with alumni teachers. My preservice teachers and I learn together as we research and plan with our community partners, just as our partners learn from us as we share ideas to support their needs. This process is integral to the stakeholder's development of democratic thinking, as it requires everyone to consider and add to the sharing of multiple viewpoints and experiences. Through active participation in art education, students construct their individual stories, see multiple perspectives illustrated through narratives of others, and build the empathy and care required for engagement in democratic practices (Gude, 2009). We all have individual perceptions of the world based on our lived experiences, but through the dialogue and learning that community art requires, we can make connections to understand the differing perspectives and beliefs of others. Reciprocity occurs when we use our understanding of others to strengthen our academic and civic learning through art making.

I continuously learn from my alumni students who are working in the field as I support them in their continued professional development. We learn together how best to communicate and collaborate and build a stronger relationship. Since they are no longer students, new roles of mentoring and support evolve as alumni become mentors for my preservice teachers. They in turn work closely with K–12 students to strengthen their growth as artists. Through community arts practices, preservice teachers are able to see firsthand the social problems in their community and how community-based art education (CBAE) allows them to understand what it feels like to become a democratic citizen through strong partnership and engaged coursework.

As an undergraduate studying art education, I attended a midwestern university whose campus was divided by a large river. The art department was housed on one side of the river and the art education department was on the other side. Due to this separation, I didn't feel at home in either department. Instead, I found myself on the periphery, navigating my way through school and my path to a career in art education. In seeking to build a sense of community, my classmates and I congregated in the former university laboratory school, in the bottom level of an old building, where art education was housed. The basement area was large, dark, lined with lockers, and frankly, a bit ominous at times, but it was where we held our Saturday morning art classes for children in the community. Due to the age of this building, there was much freedom to make this area our own. A few dedicated peers and I wrote a modest grant for acquiring materials to create a mosaic on the wall near the art education office to make the area more inviting. Our project, a ceramic-tiled children's paintbox with paint brushes, was made from real "retired" brushes, and the paint tray's lid featured swirled paint created by using found objects to represent the vivid imagination of children as they create. Working together with my classmates to develop an idea that was welcoming and shared with everyone who entered the building, I saw the impact that community art could have to transform a place, build community, and share my vision with others through art making. This experience provided me with a sense of belonging to my area of study and created long-lasting friendships with my peers, and I felt encouraged to continue this work as I became an art educator.

## COMMUNITY-BASED ART EDUCATION

When we think of the word "community," it can be divided into several components. As Congdon (2004) related, there is "community as a location or site, community as shared personal or group identification, and community as common purpose or set of beliefs" (p. 6). These components of community can play a vital role in developing one's community art practices as they help to define the focus of teaching and encourage students to develop as citizens. My approach to community art stems from the work of Lawton, Walker, and Green (2019) in community-based art education. They describe CBAE as bringing diverse groups together, based around art making and critical discussion of community issues through collaborative art making. What is empowering about CBAE is that it can bridge "art education in the classroom setting and its application in the community beyond school with demonstrable examples of how the arts impact responsible citizenship"

(p. 2). This can be transformative for all participants, creating the opportunity for both personal and community dialogue and learning.

Another strong influence on my teaching practices is from arts-based service learning (ABSL) and the work of Pamela G. Taylor and Christine Ballengee-Morris (2004) and their beliefs in the language of "we" during the development and implementation of service-learning work with their students. This "we" means that working together with a community partner, "we" must plan, learn, and reflect together within the service-learning project to ensure learning for all students, instructors, and community partners. These are factors in my approach to teaching and implementing ABSL in my practices. Critiques of service learning have raised concerns that it can reinforce privilege and power imbalance, allowing students to see themselves working with the community as more of an experiment or practice exercise, rather than a joint partnership to assist with a community's social problems. It is essential that students see service learning as both an opportunity to experience learning from the community as much as they are giving of their skills to the community. Both CBAE and ABSL are rooted in the work of Paulo Freire (1970, 1998), focusing on his belief in agency and social justice in education. Building long-enduring networks helps to mitigate the potential for a one-time, imbalanced experience for all involved.

Perhaps the best indication of the power of community art practices are those that demonstrate how they rhizomatically grow and produce more networks with every collaboration. When I work with alumni in the field, they in turn inspire their students, some of whom we see a few years later in our undergraduate program because of their transformational experience in K–12 art. The preservice teachers, in turn, learn why such experiences can be transformative, and through the support of faculty and their mentor teachers, continue to grow and spread the practice in their future classrooms. In practice, I connect preservice teachers with alumni teachers almost every semester, and complete the triangle with a community group. I plan with a local school or nonprofit organization to create a collaborative community project in which my art education students have opportunities to research, plan, and develop an art lesson based around a contemporary and timely theme in art education and grounded in a community issue or need. We have worked with various community groups, such as a local nature reserve and interpretive center, human rights organizations, and women's and youth shelters.

With each of these projects, I have developed close relationships with schools and community organizations because the alumni art teachers and community members see the importance and impact of participating in these collaborative projects. My preservice teachers learn firsthand how to research, plan, and develop art lessons about broader themes in education, while engaging closely with diverse groups of people, and see how networking, collaborating, and connecting with the community can strengthen and support their teaching practices. In the next sections, I will highlight several projects and share how I work to build community with undergraduates and graduates across the state, and continue to grow a network of actively engaged art educators.

## PRESERVICE TEACHERS GIVING BACK HOPE: BUILDING NETWORKS IN THE COMMUNITY

While simultaneously balancing my new faculty position at a university with my role as a new mother in a new community, I joined the board at a local nonprofit organization that supports women and children experiencing homelessness. This transitional housing program focuses on empowering women to learn life skills, get access to mental and physical health support, gain financial literacy, find employment, and live independently with their children. My research has focused on how civic engagement through the arts can be an alternative form of field experience for preservice teachers. I worked with the shelter to offer an after-school program for children in the transitional housing program while their moms worked on educational programming. The preservice teachers enrolled in my course learned about poverty, homelessness, and how community support can empower families as they work to overcome barriers to success. They gained new perspectives of these social issues and how they can go unseen at school. Many preservice teachers learned that homelessness may take on many forms and can be easy to overlook, all while also learning to teach art in an after school setting to multi-age groups of children experiencing trauma. We learned about laws related to homelessness and how the school district and local social supports were available to children experiencing crisis. I continued on the board at this nonprofit for 4 more years. During that time, the preservice teachers had many reciprocal opportunities to continue to learn from and support this organization.

This transitional housing program is located in a large building divided up into 15 small apartments with a playground, community room, community pantry, and staff offices. In 2017, the volunteer coordinator reached out and asked if my students and I would collaborate with the resident moms to create an artwork for the new building commemorating their successes in the program. The mothers were excited to share how they had accomplished their goals throughout their time there, and the staff wanted a creative way to celebrate their work and encourage other mothers in the program. I took this assignment to my preservice teachers, and we began to research and plan. I always include the preservice teachers in the process—indeed it is absolutely necessary to the success of the project. They must own it, too.

We first met with the service-learning librarian on campus who helped us do a deep dive into the local stats on poverty, homelessness, and school demographics. We reflected on our own encounters with and understandings of homelessness, poverty, and trauma-informed practices.

The preservice teachers brainstormed and planned out an art piece consisting of a large, framed triangle resembling a rooftop and below it, little boxes lined up together forming a square, creating the shape of a house. The words "Giving Back Hope" were spelled out in mosaic pieces within the framed triangle roof, and each graduating mom got her own box to create a mosaic within. The class of preservice teachers was divided into three groups; one created the mosaic roof, one created and painted the boxes and mosaic supplies, and one group created the teaching examples, directions, and a video to explain the process if we could not meet with each mom. Students collaborated to make sure they were communicating a unified understanding of the project, and one third of the class worked with the moms to create the first five mosaic boxes. They asked the moms ahead of time to bring an object to the workshop that represents an accomplishment they have achieved while living at the transitional housing program. These objects varied considerably, from a pocket mirror representing the ability to look at themselves and be proud of who they are, to a whistle signifying the ability to "blow the whistle on the bad things in life." Others brought more literal symbols like a toy Matchbox car to represent earning their license or buying a car, or a pencil and notepad to symbolize going to college or earning their high school diploma.

Since 2017, my students and I have completed more than 20 boxes with moms and continue to add to them each spring semester. This community art project is hung as a work in progress to continue to encourage and motivate moms to share their stories of success (Figure 10.1). I bring preservice teachers with me to help lead the workshops in order to learn

**Figure 10.1. Giving Back Wall of Hope in progress**

how art can play a powerful role in encouraging self-reflection, gratitude, and celebration. The preservice teachers share that when they visit the housing program, it helps them to understand what their future students may be encountering and encourages them to see that homelessness, poverty, and food insecurity may not always be visible to them at school.

## ALUMNA TEACHER RESTORING HOPE FOR THE FUTURE: ILLUMINATING YOUTH VOICE IN THE COMMUNITY

The 2020–2021 school year coincided with the COVID-19 pandemic, creating a challenge for community art making as large groups of people were discouraged from gathering. While this could threaten existing and possible networks, it also provided new opportunities to re-imagine art making in the era of social distancing. Collaboration and heavily populated art events were canceled, and I feared my students would miss out on a large portion of our course learning. Then I was approached with an opportunity to participate in a COVID-safe arts festival, taking place completely outdoors, and my optimism returned. I reached out to an alumna, Lacy Irwin, who had just been hired as an art teacher in a low-income urban middle school, and asked her to collaborate on this large-scale project to highlight student voices in her school during the pandemic. Because Lacy had been a student of mine just a year prior and had participated in several large community art projects, the transition from participant to facilitator seemed like a natural progression for which she was well suited.

Our goal was to capture the perspective of local middle school youth during this pandemic year through the creation of multimedia art promoting positivity and inclusivity in the community. The project was developed through a collaborative partnership between the university's Interactive Digital Studies program and Art Education program, with an urban middle school art class of majority Black and Latinx 6th-graders. Together, my preservice art teachers developed a lesson plan incorporating photography, video, drawing, and reflective writing to encourage and support the middle school students as they shared their individual hopes for the future during this difficult school year. The students photographed each other, created statements about their hope for the future, and designed and decorated face masks after narrowing their statement down to one word symbolizing their hope. We assisted them to animate their portraits and combined them together into a video. Through the creation of this multimedia art project, we were able to share these perspectives with our community by projecting them onto an outside wall of our local arts center during an event called Illuminate: Art and Light Festival (Figure 10.2). The video, as part of the festival, was played for the local community for two nights as a way to promote voices of youth and help others see how having hope during

**Figure 10.2. Images of film projected during the festival**

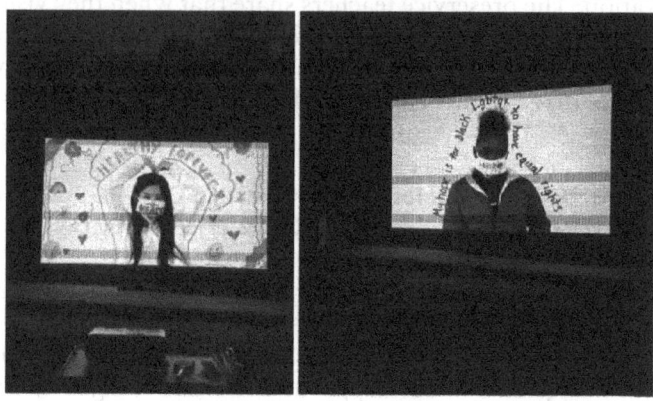

trying times can empower the promotion of positive and uplifting messages. Our project was one of 15 sites in the festival, and despite the pandemic, community members were able to safely walk through the campus and surrounding neighborhood to view the projected artworks and interact in various ways.

This collaborative opportunity communicated the voices of marginalized students and their hopes for the future to the wider community for inclusion in continued dialogues. By focusing this community artwork on "the future" rather than the difficulties of that year, it was an act of positive mindfulness and helped the students feel connected to one another and the community. As the National Youth Poet Laureate Amanda Gorman (CBS Interactive, 2020) wrote, "The question isn't if we will weather this unknown, but how we will weather this unknown together" (lines 11–12). We worked with the students to see how their voices were stronger "together." This brings back the framework of "we" and how important it was throughout this project to have the 6th-grade students as involved as possible in creating and sharing their experiences and hope for their own lives. In her 2009 Lowenfeld lecture, Olivia Gude (2009) said, "Awareness of the significance of investigating and representing experience, engaging and reworking traditions, making and sharing meaning—builds within students key habits of democratic people—freedom to experience fully, reflect freely, and represent without fear," (p. 6). By developing a lesson in which the middle school students had access to a camera to photograph one another, and were empowered to share their hopes for the future through a written statement and visual design elements of drawing and animation, we were able to represent youth voices and illuminate their hopes for the community on the walls of our local art center.

Working with Lacy was beneficial for multiple reasons: I was able to support her in a difficult time, as she took on a challenging position as a brand-new teacher in a pandemic year, while also bringing in preservice teachers to individually work with her middle school students in the art room. Although many schools across the country were not meeting in person because of the pandemic, here the principal agreed to allow us, taking the proper precautions, to come to school twice a week for several weeks because she knew how isolated her students were feeling during this time. Through these one-on-one conversations and reflective art activities both groups of students, preservice and middle school, received support for their social-emotional-learning needs.

My preservice teachers saw Lacy, a new teacher, modeling resilience and compassion for her students as they entered the art room each class period masked, in school uniforms, lugging large plastic shields that would both protect them from the virus and inadvertently isolate and divide them from their peers. Being together as a class, the preservice teachers learned how to build relationships based on how the art teacher interacted with the students and how their peers interacted, and this experience seemed to restore some excitement toward becoming a teacher while the majority of their classes were online or in hybrid format. The middle school students looked forward to our visits and opened up and shared many hopes, fears, dreams, wishes—both serious and sometimes comical. The students' personal sharing inspired the preservice teachers to work together to create a quality projection video for the festival.

## GRADUATE STUDENT CREATING RAIN BARRELS AS ECOLOGICAL ART PRACTICE

I have been fortunate enough to have some students as undergraduates who then return to complete their master's degree in our online cohort. Working with two-time alumna Ashley Cardamone, I developed an arts-based service learning (ABSL) project together with her 9th-grade students and my preservice art teachers. Because Ashley completed her action research project facilitating an ABSL project connecting a painting lesson with the local humane society (as she described in Chapter 7), I anticipated she would be enthusiastic to continue this work with her students.

Through the study of ecology and ethics of care, students in both of our classes learned about watershed ecology and its impact on our community due to recent flooding in our area (Miller & Cardamone, 2021). To begin this project, I met with a local naturalist who shared that they had a need to teach watershed ecology to school-age students but only tended to have access to elementary students in the area. This conversation about the need to raise awareness about our local environment led me to contact Ashley and invite her to work with me on this project. Through our shared interests and passion for community arts, we developed a unit guided by three goals. Our first goal was to promote care and connection to the local environment through firsthand experiences in nature, working to build an ecological identity within both groups of students (Pelo, 2013). The second goal was to help students learn through research and reflection how their actions can have a positive or negative effect on the environment by creating a collage based on their observations of nature, their research on environmental issues, and reflective thoughts on how taking action through service learning impacted them (Martusewicz et al., 2014). The third goal was to take action, raising awareness of our local environmental issues and raising funds through the creation of rain barrels, traditional water catchment systems to aid in water conservation (Miller & Cardamone, 2021).

This collaborative community art project encouraged students to learn and create together, making decorative rain barrels to help the future of their community, and discover how art making can help provide sustainable ways to address ecological challenges related to their local environment. In order for students to apply their understanding of this larger issue, we designed a curricular unit so students could explore environmental issues in which they were interested, examine how human impact is affecting the local ecosystem, create opportunities to develop care for the environment, and use art making to educate local community members. We layered student learning through art making and reflective activities, took a field trip to a nature reserve, and then completed the rain barrels by stenciling images inspired by our nature visit (Figure 10.3). The rain barrel decorations were designed to document learning from the trip, allow students to express their environmental concerns, and continue conversations about environmental

**Figure 10.3. Rain barrel stenciling in progress**

issues in the future (Miller & Cardamone, 2021). Last, we auctioned off the rain barrels at a benefit to fund renovations at the interpretive center. New knowledge was gained, and we were able to raise awareness for water conservation and soil run-off, while also creating beautifully stenciled artwork in small groups led by preservice teachers. I saw evidence of empowerment as students recognized their responsibility to care for the environment, and preservice teachers recognized their ability to facilitate these projects within their own classrooms.

Collaborating with Ashley, I was able to strengthen the network connection by deepening our teacher–student relationship twice, and as co-collaborator on this ABSL project. Our shared experience of making rain barrels together connected networks of students, while also further expanding those networks for future students and future colleagues.

## LESSONS LEARNED AND SHARED: BUILDING AND MAINTAINING CONNECTIONS

Each of the projects I share here connected deeply to one of the three components of "community." Additionally, each reflected the importance of "we" in my approach to community art as well as the need for change, personal or community/societal. When creating "Giving Back Hope," we focused on caring for the needs in our community by examining challenging social issues in our local community that affect the well-being of children and their families and how that impacts their learning. We worked to understand the challenges single mothers face and the adversities children will bring to school.

Our "Hope for the Future" project provided opportunity for preservice teachers to connect with local urban youth whose voices have historically been marginalized; together we worked to share important issues about economics, health, sexual identity, race, and equal rights with our local community. This opportunity to elevate a variety of students' cultural identities raised awareness, built a sense of belonging, and allowed all community viewers to learn what is important to our youth.

Lastly, for our rain barrel project, we again look at social and environmental issues in our own community and how we can take action as citizens to help reduce soil runoff, conserve water, and care for our local watershed. Working with the students for a month allowed us to make art and reflect on their beliefs. We asked the students to consider, "Do you belong to the Earth, or does the Earth belong to you?" (Miller & Cardamone, 2021). In our final reflection with the 9th-grade students, many of their views had moved from believing that responsibility for caring for local water belongs to "everyone" or someone else, to believing that the responsibility is "mine" (personal communication with students, 2017).

Over the last 14 years, I have been engaging my preservice teachers in the local community, working with school and community organizations, and connecting with other departments on campus. I see the benefits of this work when my alumni reach out to continue working with me after they become practicing teachers throughout our state and even internationally. Teachers see how community art projects assist them in better understanding community demographics and the social issues their students and families are facing. Both alumnae teachers highlighted in this chapter, Ashley and Lacy, have gone on to incorporate community art lessons into their curricula through service learning, collaborative art making, and murals. They, among many other graduates of our department, continue to strengthen their teaching by connecting with the community and growing their roots in community art-making approaches. This collaborative work prepares their own K–12 students to practice being involved in their community, allowing them to see that they have a place and voice within their community and can be contributing citizens who use art to make a positive impact on the people in their lives.

## REFERENCES

CBS Interactive. (2020, April 17). Youth Poet Laureate Amanda Gorman offers words of hope amid coronavirus pandemic. *CBS News*. Retrieved October 12, 2022, from https://www.cbsnews.com/news/amanda-gorman-youth-poet-laureate-coronavirus-pandemic/

Congdon, K. G. (2004). *Community art in action*. Davis Publishing.

Freire, P. (1970). *Pedagogy of the oppressed*. Herder and Herder.

Freire, P. (1998). *Pedagogy of freedom: Ethics, democracy and civic courage*. Rowman & Littlefield.

Gude, O. (2009). The 2009 Lowenfeld lecture: Art education for democratic life. *Art Education, 62*(6), 6–11.

Lawton, P. H., Walker, M. A., & Green, M. (2019). *Community-based art education across the lifespan: Finding common ground*. Teachers College Press.

Martusewicz, R. A., Edmundson, J., & Lupinacci, J. (2014). *Ecojustice education: Toward diverse, democratic, and sustainable communities*. Routledge.

Miller, W., & Cardamone, A. (2021). Educating through art, ecology, and ecojustice: A rain barrel project. *Art Education, 74*(1), 40–45.

Pelo, A. (2013). *The goodness of rain: Developing an ecological identity in young children*. Exchange Press.

Taylor, P. G., & Ballengee-Morris, C. (2004). Service-learning a language of "we." *Art Education, 57*(5), 6–12.

AFTERWORD

# Defending the Useless
## A Neighborhood in Flux

*Jeff Rufus Byrd*

In March 2020, I was Head of the Department of Art at the University of Northern Iowa when COVID-19 forced my campus to close. My calendar suddenly filled with frantic meetings as administrators tried to figure out how to move forward. I had used Zoom on occasion before, but very few of my colleagues had even heard of it. Panic was everywhere as we considered such practical matters as how ceramics could be taught without a kiln and how science courses would proceed without a lab. It was disappointing to find that all the talk of "creative problem solving," so much a part of college recruitment rhetoric, simply vanished in the presence of an actual problem. I knew it would not be easy, but I had faith in my colleagues in the arts. Let's face it, we know how to use imagination to make beauty from trash.

I attended online meetings with a national group of art department chairs to brainstorm about teaching studio courses online. Everyone looked exhausted. Some ideas were presented from time to time, but we generally talked about how we could keep it together while being pulled in so many directions. At times, I felt like Oracle. For non-comic geeks, she is a member of the Batman team—a computer whiz in a wheelchair who serves as a locus of information, guidance, and encouragement for her partners in the field. I tried to do just that for all the faculty, students, and fellow admins who were calling, texting, and emailing with questions large and small.

We carried on, and it was, in fact, possible to teach ceramics without a kiln. Apparently, clay is everywhere! Printmaking jumped into DIY mode with stencils and spray paint. Sculpture found materials and spaces to assemble them in. Painting and drawing students got personalized instruction and individual critiques. Performance art students staged their first livestream showcases. Once Adobe unlocked everyone's accounts, photography and graphic design were business as usual. To be clear: None of this was easy. But we carried on.

But the challenges of rethinking how a university works were only compounded by fear of the unknown world that was unfolding. The news was frightening. Restaurants, bars, and theaters closed. Sports teams played in empty arenas. The barren streets looked like some science fiction movie where everyone had suddenly vanished. Even the wind sounded empty.

There were more and more messages from students requesting meetings. It was usually about some course requirement or if I knew how long the campus would be closed. In most cases, they just wanted someone to talk to. It was reassuring that the technology was in place, and we could chat about art like things were normal. They were back home from college in their high school bedrooms, and I knew this had to be a strange experience for them.

Conversely, experiencing everything through a screen has a kind of numbing effect that I had never experienced. I call it sensory monotony. It's about seeing and watching while the other senses are left out. I looked for ways to escape. Whenever there was a break in the ongoing meetings, I would make a sandwich and get into my car and drive somewhere. Everything was closed and late winter was too chilly to sit outside. There wasn't much to see through my car's front window, but I would find trees or water or architectural details on buildings—anything real to look at. I came to realize I was swapping one type of screen for another.

My husband and I were lucky in that we could continue to work from home and were at less risk for infection. However, when you work from home and there's nowhere to go after work . . . does the work ever actually end?

We began walking the dog at least three, sometimes even four, times a day. This was a turning point. I have lived in the same house for 27 years but had never actually explored the neighborhood. We became more familiar with the world right outside our own door. It was exactly what I needed, a far more effective means of escaping the screen and relieving the sensory monotony.

Everyone else seemed to be out walking too, and we chatted with neighbors we had never met. We waved at the older ladies who gathered in their winter parkas at the picnic tables in the park. All six feet apart. We met all the dogs too; learned when the owls are out; and discovered there's a flock of turkeys that make their way through the neighborhood every day. In the evenings, they bed down (or up as it were) in tall trees in a ravine. Since they don't fly well, it's quite funny to watch how they get there.

To honor the dogs in our extended neighborhood pack, I'd like to give them a shout-out: Greg and Susan McFlurry (who belong to us), Oakie, Red, Ella, Daisy, Monk, Lucy, Jay-C, Chance, Windu, Molly, Millie, Zena, Lexie, Molly 2, Leggy Dog, Other Dog (okay . . . we can never remember those last two dogs' names, but you must admit those are pretty good substitutes; we remember the names of the owners even less!).

Early on, I started to notice teddy bears in the windows of a couple of houses. In the following days, more and more bears appeared. We joined in by placing a Mr. Spock bear in our front window.

# Afterword

The many small children in our neighborhood were also going on walks with their parents. I'm sure the pandemic was tough on them, being stuck at home away from playmates and grandparents. I imagined the bears were fun for them to see and count as they walked around. It made things a little less scary. There was one particular bear with a goofy smile that always made me feel a little lighter. What I don't remember is ever getting a memo that we were all going to start displaying bears in our windows. Only recently, I learned that the bear hunt trend was based on a popular children's book (McCluskey, 2020). At the time, it appeared to be spontaneous. I suspect others were like me and simply joined because it seemed like the right thing to do. That small collective gesture indicated we were all thinking of others.

Later, I began noticing painted rocks hidden here and there. Some had inspirational messages like "You rock!" and "Peace." I was aware that these could be purchased online, but what I saw had a funkier kid-art vibe. I was happy someone was using the lockdown to make art. As with the bears, I was surprisingly moved by these rocks. It hit me that someone intuitively knew it was worth their time to paint messages and send them out into the world on the off-chance a stranger might find one at just the right moment, making a small but genuine impact.

Did those rocks end the pandemic? No. But they gave me the boost I needed to go back into another meeting and help someone else in whatever way that I could. They sent out ripples.

As the months passed, creativity blossomed in the neighborhood. Although social distancing was still the norm, everyone gratefully welcomed the warmer weather. One family treated the block to a parade with wagons, red balloons, and all five kids in animal costumes waving flags and blowing soap bubbles. A secretary from the Math Department set up a television in her garage and held Zumba classes in her driveway. Someone created a kooky assemblage featuring a 3-foot John Cena doll balancing on a traffic cone. Sadly, it was stolen.

One neighbor's collection of inflatable snowman sculptures set off a lawn ornament trend that we eventually joined. We already had a display of small dinosaur figures, then dragons appeared, and those were followed by plastic flamingos. Our flock is now 50-strong in all colors. We arranged and dressed them for all the major holidays. They looked a bit like scenes from a Busby Berkeley musical. The flamingos were a big hit, with many neighbors stopping to say how much they enjoyed them. During one walk, a mostly housebound neighbor brought out a flamingo painting she had done! She was holding it upside-down when she presented it to us, so that is how it is now exhibited in our home.

Our most popular lawn setups were staged races between four of the flamingos with little action figures glued on top as jockeys. The daily moves were determined by dice rolls so the winner was always a surprise. Chewbacca the jockey was a fan favorite. Unfortunately, he never won.

In fall, a tree died and had to be cut down. We found that it had died of a fungus, so we put up an informative display about dendrochronology, inviting passersby to come up and count the rings on the stump.

At Halloween, several folks invented clever low-contact ways of distributing candy using makeshift clotheslines or arrangements on tables or chairs that would be refilled as the candy was taken. When winter hit, another neighbor built a small ice rink in his front yard so his young daughter could learn to skate. It was shaped like a king-sized mattress and illuminated from below. At night, it glowed beautifully against the snow.

All of this was surprising, joyful, fun, and filled with a scrappy spirit to break through the looming fear and anxiety of the pandemic. Mostly it was just kind and giving.

But was it art? That all depends on what you are open and willing to accept as art.

Fluxus was an international group of artists who, in the 1960s, set out to expand the notion of art. Based on the principle that art is a thought rather than an object, Fluxus is perhaps the most democratic of all art movements. Most pieces are brief and often ambiguous sets of instructions called event scores. These are free and most require no specific skills. Kristine Stiles (1993) states, "Scores may be performed in the mind as a thought, or in the body with a physical action. They may be performed in public or in private, by an individual or a collective" (p. 67).

One of my favorite event scores is Alison Knowles's *Identical Lunch* (1968), which simply reads "a tuna fish sandwich on wheat toast with butter and lettuce, no mayo, and a cup of soup or glass of buttermilk." This piece reminds me of rituals like the Japanese tea ceremony. Performing it slows you down. I always carefully inspect each item on the menu as I assemble the meal. I try to find a genuinely pretty piece of lettuce. I spread the tuna carefully, trying not to damage the bread. The ironic thing about this piece is that it's often difficult to follow exactly. I don't like how butter tastes with tuna, so I cheat and add a little mayo. And yes, I always go for the buttermilk. When I assign this to students, they often try to order it at a restaurant and find it's possible to get some, but rarely all, of the ingredients.

Yoko Ono, also a member of the Fluxus group, created many event scores that connected simple actions with larger ideas. In 2021–2022, London's Whitechapel Gallery presented a version of Ono's *Mend Piece* (1966/2018) that eerily linked to the crisis we were slowly emerging from. Gallery goers were presented with a range of broken cups and plates on a white table along with glue, tape, scissors, and string. The score: "Mend carefully. Think of mending the world at the same time." While the activity itself is engaging, Ono states "it's not mending the cup so much as what you think about while you're mending it" (Scarth, 2021, 10:27). Trying to "mend the world" seems like an impossible task, but Ono's piece suggests that mending one small thing might start the process. Art therapist

# Afterword

Nicky Roland notes the importance of mindfulness to healing and self-care and sees *Mend Piece* as ideal for anyone who is anxious about making art because they do not know what to make. Since the broken pieces "can't go back to what they were . . . there's got to be a new creation" (Scarth, 2021, 12:39).

I performed *Mend Piece* with M.A. art education students in the 2022 spring semester. They were working teachers taking my online class. We were all under stress strictly adhering to various safety procedures in the classroom. This stress was compounded by the fact that state politicians were lambasting teachers with complaints about a number of hot-button issues. So, we sat together on Zoom, smashed some cups, and tried to put them together again. This was the first time I had performed this piece. I thought it would be easy, but it took precise concentration. I moved slowly and carefully since my cup broke into pointy, sharp shards. Save for tinkling noises, our virtual space was silent as we focused on the task.

Afterwards, everyone agreed that it was a calming experience. One student described how the task pushed other thoughts out of her mind. Another mentioned it was good to take a break from worrying about tomorrow's classes. When I sent out a survey asking them to rate the projects we did in class, several mentioned *Mend Piece* as being particularly meaningful. One said, "It was very meditative, and I really needed it at this time."

Personally, I think this performance helped me make peace with being back in front of a screen again.

While my neighbors and I were not responding to a score, I believe our spontaneous actions during the shutdown were very much in the character of Fluxus. George Maciunas, who coordinated many Fluxus events, describes it as "against art as a medium for the artist's ego . . . and tends toward the spirit of the collective" (Stiles, 1993, p. 69). But again, can we look at eating a sandwich or gluing a cup together or arranging lawn flamingos as art?

As a performance artist, I'm quite accustomed to that question. In my work and in my teaching, I embrace several concepts that many people find challenging to see as art. Not because they are specifically offensive, but rather that they seem too easy. Once, in a meeting, a fellow department head said to me, "If I can do it, I don't consider it art." Oddly, he repeated that sentence again in the same conversation. I've heard this sentiment expressed often with reference to children and the scribbles and drips of painters like Jackson Pollock or Cy Twombly. In those cases, I generally think that the person hasn't looked closely at the work of either artist or at the work of children. Engagement with art takes time. We live in a culture where people are taught to label and categorize rather than actually see and experience something.

Ultimately, this attitude is tragic. It closes a person off to many experiences simply because they believe that certain skills and knowledge of technique are the baseline for identifying something as art. This rigidity is restricting and potentially problematic. As children, we all draw, dance, and sing. But most give it up once they believe they are not good at it. At this point, they leave art to the professionals and go into consumer mode. But even for those consumers, art is seen as a luxury . . . if it's seen at all.

In June 2020, Singapore's *Sunday Times* published an infographic outlining the results of a poll asking people to rank the jobs they considered to be most essential and most nonessential during the pandemic (Tan, 2020). We had just learned the phrase "essential workers," even though everyone was acting as if that concept had been around forever, so such a poll seemed strange. Still, it was no surprise that doctors and nurses shared the most-essential slot. The next two slots were custodians and garbage collectors. Normally, it would be surprising to see the latter two positions within the top five "most essential," but the pandemic ushered in a newfound appreciation for previously undervalued jobs.

It was, however, the top nonessential jobs that gave me pause—artist and telemarketer. The second-place winner was a surprise because I didn't know that job still existed; very few people will answer a call from an unknown number. But, considering so many of us had just wrapped ourselves in the warm blanket of streaming media, I was taken aback to see artist topping the list. With everything shut down, there was little news to report outside of the pandemic. It seemed everywhere you looked there were lists of books, movies, music, and television shows to check out and immerse oneself in. Yet, this survey seemed to indicate that no artists were needed.

Granted, there was immediate pushback to the *Sunday Times* poll, so much so that the market research company that ran the survey felt the need to respond (Tracy, 2020). Many of those voicing concerns quoted author Mo Willems, "Science will get us out of this. But art will get us through this." However, those coming to the defense of the arts were primarily artists and designers themselves. So, I doubt the conversation went much beyond that bubble.

In my job, I've given countless recruitment tours and met with many potential students and their parents. Over time, I realized that much art is simply invisible. When most people see photographs, advertisements, book covers, websites, packages, movie posters, music videos, or even infographics, they do not see the person or team who made it. Parents were likewise surprised to hear we had alumni who work in film and television—artists who design and make sets, props, costumes, title sequences, animations, and storyboards for action scenes. We live in a visual world and yet few wonder, "Who makes it?"

While many parents of prospective art students are supportive, others regarded their children's interest in art as something akin to a terminal disease. (My own mother cried when I told her I was majoring in art, and this was way before anyone had ever heard of STEM.) Art is generally seen as a useless endeavor. When I proudly told one family of a prospective student about our high job-placement rates, the father said he simply didn't believe me. Another parent made it clear to me her son was not permitted to major in art. He was visibly upset, so I mentioned it's possible to major in something else and minor in art. With a withering glance, she asked, "Do you think that's responsible?"

I completely understand that students need to make a living and that future debt weighs heavily on them. But I also understand the truth underneath cartoonist and MacArthur Genius Fellow Lynda Barry's dark joke: "Art is a public health concern because it keeps you from killing yourself and others" (Marchese, 2022). When my neighbors and I engaged in all those useless yet fun and inspired activities during the pandemic, it was something we needed to do. Is it responsible to ignore our need for peace, connection, humor, play, and kindness?

Kristine Stiles (1993) states, "Fluxus performances existed in a social space and their resonance continues in that lived space" (p. 65). I think our ongoing interactions as neighbors is that resonance. It took a global pandemic for us to break away from the utilitarian thinking that haunts American lives.

It has become a challenge to see things with no market value as still having value. For Barry (2008), this mindset is a problem, especially in relation to mental health. The solution is reframing art as a process of imaginative engagement with the world, not as manipulation of certain materials. It's play, which has often been dismissed as entertainment. For Barry, play is a particular state of mind. She says, "At the center of everything we call 'the arts' and children call 'play' is something which seems somehow alive" (p. 14). Only recently have I reconnected with this aliveness as an adult. My husband and I have collaborated on the creation of a family of puppets since first meeting 20 years ago. He was working as a Blackboard administrator and very active in the community of ITS professionals who used the application. Attending the annual conference with him in 2003, I discovered he was a bit of a celebrity. He began using a sheepdog puppet, Winston, on social media posts and other interactions with the community. It was clear they were hungry for play and Winston became an even bigger celebrity.

After he left that job, we continued to add puppets: Elton the lion, Sebastian the tiger, and, most recently, Phelix Pheltfinger, a fuzzy monster with a constant panicky expression. Over time each has developed a complex inner life that I think encapsulates what Barry refers to as "alive." Winston is a sunny optimist who gets breathlessly excited over just about anything. Elton is more laid back and mellow. Phelix is an orphan with a hyper-religious foster mom. He recently discovered he was a puppet. The experience was not unlike my own coming-out process in college.

The puppets are part of our "responsible" lives. They travel with us as we visit museums and other places. We post short videos of them, and we have a whole slate of running jokes about how they experience the world. For example: Winston has seen very few movies, so he is completely blown away by well-known endings like the one in Planet of the Apes. We laugh when we act out how he would try to share his excitement without giving away the surprise. We're seeing a worn-out trope with innocent eyes.

I've known several fiction writers who speak of a point in their writing process when their characters begin making decisions and taking actions that the authors did not anticipate until the moment of the writing. I think of the puppets in this way. I even worry about their happiness and well-being. For example, Sebastian has been afraid of magicians for several years. He had an orange watch that he was very proud of, but sadly lost. Soon after, he saw a magician on television who made someone's watch disappear and became convinced this was how his old watch vanished. It then made him fearful this would happen to his new one. On a recent trip to Las Vegas, we took Sebastian to see a live magic show hoping to alleviate his fears. I don't think it worked because (no joke) the magician borrowed a watch from someone in the audience and made it disappear!

I have never written this down before. When I contemplate you reading it, I feel a wave of embarrassment. Why is that? Why does engaging with the world in an imaginative way seem so uncomfortable to share? Why do I care? I am a performance artist, so most everyone thinks I'm nuts anyway. What does it matter if I've got some puppets and flamingos riding on my crazy train? But sharing this information seems like a step too far. Clearly, the world has taught me to think this is useless, irresponsible, and shameful.

Even now, it's a challenge to silence that inner critic. Has society planted in us a conformity control device called embarrassment? But there are times you must ask, "What has embarrassment ever done for me?" If the puppets afford me the chance to see the world anew, how can that be useless?

To be clear, my defense of the useless is not an argument for a de-professionalization of the arts. I still enjoy seeing and hearing the work of artists who have mastered their craft. I simply ask that we expand our concept of art to provide encouragement, permission, and freedom for everyone to approach life with greater openness and playfulness so they may experience that aliveness.

Art can happen anywhere at any time. And it should. This is the responsible thing to do.

So, how about making art now?
An event score:

Look at the list of dogs a few pages back.
Pick one and try to imagine what that dog might look like.
Are they big or small? What color and how long is the fur?
Draw a picture of this dog.
Give the dog a jaunty hat.

Then make a sandwich, tuna optional.

## REFERENCES

Barry, L. (2008). *What it is*. Drawn & Quarterly.
McCluskey, M. (2020). "It's like a silent visual message." How social distancing-friendly "bear hunts" are uniting neighborhoods amid coronavirus. *Time*. https://time.com/5809613/bear-hunts-coronavirus/
Marchese, D. (2022, September 2). A genius cartoonist believes child's play is anything but frivolous. *The New York Times Magazine*.
Scarth, J. (2021, August 25). Yoko Ono: MEND PIECE for London (No. 11). In *Hear, Now*. Whitechapel Gallery. https://whitechapelgallery.org/exhibitions/yoko-ono-mend-piece-for-london/
Stiles, K. (1993). *In the spirit of Fluxus*. Walker Art Center.
Tan, A. (2020). Sunday Times survey saying artist is topmost non-essential job sparks anger in community. *Mothership*. https://mothership.sg/2020/06/sunday-times-survey-artist-non-essential/
Tracy, S. (2020). Milieu insight response and clarification on the Sunday Times essential workers poll. *Milieu*. https://www.mili.eu/insights/sunday-times-essential-workers-poll-response

# Index

ABSL. *See* Arts-Based Service Learning
Advocacy, 5, 86–97, 115
Anderson, T., 29
Animals, 16–19, 22–23, 80, 113–120, 122–126, 145
Arctic Circle, 17
Arts-Based Service Learning (ABSL), 152, 157, 159

Ballengee-Morris, Christine, 152
Bandura, Albert, 50, 55, 58–59, 99
Barry, Lynda, 116, 167
Behaviors, 16, 54, 76, 100, 102. *See also* Classroom management
Berglas, S., 99, 106
Bergmann, J., 49
Berry, Barb, 34
Blackboard, 167
Blatt-Gross, Carolina, 127, 133–134, 138, 141
Bloom's Taxonomy, 4
Brown, Brené, 127, 134, 137–138
Bryant, J., 86–87
Buffington, M. L., 87, 97, 114–115, 117

Canvas Learning System. *See* Learning Management System
CBAE. *See* Community-Based Art Education
Care ethics. *See* Ethics of care
Centers, 29–34
Choice-based curriculum and pedagogy, 5, 26–31, 35, 38, 41–42, 47
Chromebook, 49
Civic engagement, 128, 153. *See also* Democratic engagement

Classroom
  management, 27, 49, 54, 67. *See also* Behaviors
  structure, 5, 14, 24
Collaborative art, 17, 140–142, 147, 150–151, 160. *See also* Collaborative learning
Collaborative learning, 56
Community art, 5–6, 90, 110, 127–134, 137–138, 140–141, 150–152, 154–160
Community-Based Art Education (CBAE), 151–152
Congdon, K., 109, 151
Conservation, 81, 158–159
Convention on Rights of the Child, 85
Cooper, M., 142
Corona virus. *See* COVID-19
COVID-19, 1, 44, 50, 56, 60, 102–103, 128, 132, 155, 161
Creative bank account, 69–70, 73, 77–80, 83
Creativity, 4, 27, 29–30, 41–42, 74, 94, 113, 127–128, 137–138, 163
Culturally responsive pedagogy. *See* Culturally sustaining pedagogy
Culturally sustaining pedagogy, 4

Daniels, S., 86–87
Democracy, 1–2, 6–7, 9–10, 63–64, 110–142
Dewey, John, 2, 7, 9, 63–34, 109–110, 127, 131, 133–134
Dewhurst, Marit, 2
Differentiation, 44, 47, 67, 79
Digital portfolios, 69, 71–74, 79, 83
Diversity, 7, 33, 110, 130–132, 134, 136–137, 145

Drostle, Gary, 143
Dugan, Jamila, 4

Efland, Arthur, 28–29
ELL. *See* English Language Learners
Empathy, 3, 5, 13–15, 20, 22–23, 25, 38, 113–115, 124–125, 150
Empty Bowls, 114
Engagement
 civic, 128, 153
 democratic, 6, 9, 127, 130–131, 137
 student, 31, 47, 68, 122
English Language Learners (ELL), 16, 47, 49, 88, 102, 148
Essaydi, Lalla, 33
Ethics of care, 110, 114, 121, 125, 157

Felleman-Fattal, L. R., 86–87
Flipgrid, 102–103
Flipped learning, 46, 48, 56
Fluxus, 164, 167
Freedman, K., 10
Freire, Paulo, 9, 152
Fritzgerald, Andratesha, 4
Fulton, K. P., 49

Gilligan, Carol, 2
Goals
 student, 3, 45, 57–58, 64, 94–95, 109–110, 117–118, 153
 teacher, 1, 3, 29, 53, 158
Google
 Classroom, 79
 Docs, 128
 Drive, 79
 Forms, 69
 Slides, 69, 79
Gorman, Amanda, 156
Green, 151
Greene, Maxine, 2, 7
Gude, Olivia, 2, 6–7, 9, 27, 29, 63–64, 109, 127, 129, 134, 150, 156

Handicapping, 99–100, 102, 106
Haraway, Donna, 2
Hathaway, N. E., 27–30
Heise, D., 10
Hetland, L., 68

Hillery, G., 127
hooks, bell, 2–4
Huard, M., 14–15
Humane society, 110, 113, 116–120, 122, 124–125, 157
Humane Society of the United States, 113
Hutzel, K., 141

Identity, 5, 27–28, 31, 33–39, 41–42, 63, 110, 141, 158–159
Individualized Education Plan (IEP), 16, 53, 102
Interactive Digital Studies (IDS), 155
iPads, 16–18
iPods, 49

Jaquith, D. B., 27–30
Jones, E., 99, 106
Journaling, 5, 34, 64, 67–70, 76, 83, 99, 102, 104–105
Journals, 69–70, 75, 78–79, 83–84

Kaizena, 69, 79, 83
Khan Academy, 48
Kindergarten, 16, 28, 30, 39, 49
Knowles, Alison, 164
Krensky, B., 115

Lage, M. J., 48
Lawton, P., 129, 151
Learning Management System (LMS), 48, 54, 60
Learning Standards, 21st Century, 44
Learning styles, 31, 48, 51–52, 55–58
Lowe, S., 127, 129–130
Lowenfeld, Viktor, 67, 156
Lundy, L., 86

Maciunas, George, 165
Meaning making, 4, 6–7, 10, 15–16, 27, 29–30, 41, 64, 74, 77, 79, 92, 135, 156
Milbrandt, M., 29
Mosaic, 6, 111, 139, 141–154
Motivation. *See* Student motivation

Murals, 6, 80, 82, 90, 110, 127–130, 132, 134–135, 137, 139, 140, 142, 150, 160

Noddings, Nel, 2, 15, 110, 113–115, 121, 125, 127, 134, 141

Obama, Barack, 85
Olly and Suzi, 17–19
Ono, Yoko, 164

Parker, Jake, 70
PBS (Public Broadcasting System), 17–18
Peer
  collaboration, 5, 14, 25, 37–38, 42
  conversation, 13–15, 25, 37, 56
  discussions, 105
  feedback, 23
  interactions, 95, 99
  monitoring, 6
  relationships, 20
Pejac, 17
Perseverance, 5–6, 74, 100–102. *See also* Resilience
Perseverant grit, 101
Phillips, L., 15
Pinterest, 67
Pollock, Jackson, 165
Preservice teachers, 1, 111, 150, 152–155, 157, 159–160
Prettyman, S., 86
Project Zero, 68
Public art, 127, 129. *See also* Community art
PBS (Public Broadcasting System), 17–18
Puppets, 167–168

QuickTime, 79

Rain barrels, 157–159
Resilience, 7, 53–54, 58–59, 157. *See also* Perseverance
Robson, Aurora, 16–17
Roehl, A., 48
Roland, Nicky, 165
Rural schools, 3, 5–6, 27, 31

Safir, Shane, 4
Sams, A., 49
Sartre, Jean-Paul, 7
Scaffolded instruction, 44, 47, 59. *See also* Scaffolding
Scaffolding, 28, 44, 47, 53–54, 67, 83, 101, 124. *See also* Scaffolded instruction
SEL. *See* Social Emotional Learning
Serriere, S. C., 86–87
Service learning, 5, 87, 110, 113–117, 120–121, 124–125, 152–153, 157–158, 160. *See also* Arts-Based Service Learning
Sheridan, K., 68
Sjostrom, L., 142
Sketchbook, sketchbooks, 16–17, 19–20, 69–71, 73–75, 77, 80, 83–84, 89–90, 93–94, 103, 116, 142, 144, 182
Slick, Duane, 33
Social Emotional Learning, 157, 182
Steffen, S. L., 115
Stiles, Kristine, 164
Student
  choice, 5, 9–11, 27, 35, 41, 52, 63, 67, 86
  motivation, 5, 45, 73, 84, 87. *See also* Engagement
  reflection, 78
  reflections, 34, 99, 124. *See also* Student reflection.
  voice, 1, 5, 27, 30, 64, 85–89, 94–97, 122, 142
Studio Habits of Mind, 5, 64, 67–69, 74, 83, 182
Suburban school, 5
Szekely, G., 14

TAB. *See* Teaching for Artistic Behavior
Taylor, Pamela G., 152
Teaching for Artistic Behavior (TAB), 26, 29
Technology, 79–80, 102, 162
Themes (in art), 5, 10, 16, 26–28, 31, 33–35, 38–42, 73–74, 76, 92, 121
Thomas, Alma Woodsey, 103
Twombly, Cy, 165

United States, 85, 113, 131
Universal Design, 4
Urban school, 5–6

Van Gogh, Vincent, 33
Veenema, S. A., 68
Vermillion, Emily, 139

Walker, M. A., 151
Warhol, Andy, 33

Wigglesworth, Ron, 100
Willems, Mo, 166
Winner, E., 68
World Wildlife Fund (WWF), 16

YouTube, 48, 70, 80

Zoom, 128, 130, 137, 161, 165

# About the Editor and the Contributors

***Dr. Elizabeth Sutton*** is professor of art history and head of the Department of Art at the University of Northern Iowa. Her scholarship, while specializing in issues of globalization and power in art and in art history, also has included active pedagogical research. Her current interests include various interdisciplinary projects that seek to amplify feminist research, methodology, and pedagogy.

***Elizabeth S. Bloomburg*** is an elementary art teacher in Johnston, Iowa. She has her bachelor's and master's degrees in art education from the University of Northern Iowa and is in her 12th year teaching. Liz is president of the Art Educators of Iowa.

***Jeff Rufus Byrd*** is a performance and video artist who has presented work in 16 countries across four continents. His writing has been published in the journals *Performance Research, Femme Salée,* and *Live Art Almanac* and in a monograph on the work of performance artist Marilyn Arsem. He has taught at the University of Northern Iowa for 33 years.

***Ashley M. Cardamone*** is a secondary art teacher in Cedar Falls, Iowa. She has taught junior high and high school art for over 10 years, and has received awards for outstanding teaching, including the Gold Star Teacher Award from the McElroy Trust in 2018 and the Yager Exemplary Teaching Recognition Award from the University of Northern Iowa in 2019.

***Kathryn Christensen*** is a middle school teacher in Denison, Iowa. She has taught high school art for over 20 years and received the Middle School Art Teacher of the Year Award in 2021 from Art Educators of Iowa.

***Michelle Cox*** is an elementary art educator in the Iowa City Community School District. She has been teaching art and working with children for over 15 years. Michelle earned a Master of Arts from the University of Northern Iowa in 2019 and a Bachelor of Fine Arts from Eastern Illinois University in 1993. Her primary focus is on community and collaborative work with her students.

***Jodi Fenton*** graduated from Iowa State University with a BA in Curriculum & Instruction (K–6) and an endorsement in Art Education (K–8) in 2000. She received her MA in Art Education (K–12) from the University of Northern Iowa in 2021. She has taught in the Des Moines Public School district for 21 years. When not teaching, she enjoys life at home and in the community.

***Dr. Samantha Goss*** is an assistant professor at the University of Northern Iowa, where she teaches secondary art methods, history of design, and various art education and research courses in the graduate art education program. Her research interest includes engrossment in various contexts. She enjoys collaboration in both teaching and research, which lead to work on art education research history through citation network analysis and data visualization.

***Maddison O. Maddock*** is an elementary art teacher just outside of Des Moines, Iowa. She has a master's degree in art education from the University of Northern Iowa and has been teaching for 13 years. Maddison currently serves as the co-mentoring and advocacy chair for the Art Educators of Iowa and the Iowa Alliance for Arts Education.

***Dr. Wendy Miller*** is associate professor of art education and is the coordinator of undergraduate art education at the University of Northern Iowa. Her research focuses on community art education, working to engage with local communities in art making through projects involving her current and former art education students.

***Sandra C. Nyberg*** is in her 12th year of teaching elementary art in central Iowa. She continues to explore ways that art education can be employed to promote Social Emotional Learning (SEL) and play. Her primary focus is that her young artists enter their studio feeling loved, known, capable, and heard.

***Lauren Roush*** is an artist and middle school art teacher, serving on the board of various nonprofit organizations focused on enriching the community of Newton, Iowa, through art. Her interests are in community involvement through art and the catharsis that art provides, and her work usually reflects concepts revolving around human connections.

***Heather Walker*** is an artist as well as an art educator. She is active in practicing pottery, watercolor, ink, and drawing. Her professional practice is centered around the Studio Habits of Mind, emphasizing the importance of practice, a growth mindset, and keeping a sketchbook. She also strives to help students personally connect to the artwork they create and see the relevance of art in their daily lives. She shares her passion for art by teaching secondary students, adult education classes, and ceramics classes at Ellsworth Community College.